10632750
RP
MORNING!
CHIRP チュン
チュン CHIRP
GOOD MORNING!
AHHH... THE SUN IS SO...
GOOD MORNING!
SO... BRIGHT...
THIS IS TERRIBLE WEATHER WE'RE HAVING.

WE VAMPIRES CAN REALLY TAKE A BEATING WHEN IT COMES TO THE SUMMER SUN, EH?
DON'T YOU THINK THERE'S BEEN AN AWFUL *LOT* OF SUNNY DAYS THIS SUMMER?
NAH... THERE WERE WAY MORE DURING THE OIL SHORTAGE IN THE SUMMER OF '73.
OH, RIGHT... THAT YEAR WAS *TOTALLY* LAME.
WASN'T THERE THAT ONE YEAR TOO, WITH THE MARCO POLO BRIDGE INCIDENT? LOT OF HOT DAYS THAT SUMMER.
AH, YES. THAT YEAR, TOO, WAS LAME.
AND THEN THERE WAS THAT SUMMER WHEN YOU GOT HOOKED ON TAYAMA KATAI, AND WE ACTUALLY TRAVELED TO MEET HIM.
AHHH... THE TAISHO ERA. NOW THAT SUMMER *REALLY* SUCKED.

SEVEN SEAS ENTERTAINMENT PRESENTS

My Pathetic Vampire Life

SBYA

story and art by **ISHIKAWA ROSE** vol. 1

TRANSLATION
Amber Tamosaitis

ADAPTATION
Carol Fox

LETTERING
Rina Mapa

LOGO DESIGN
Karis Page

COVER DESIGN
Nicky Lim

PROOFREADER
Lee Otter
Janet Houck

PRODUCTION MANAGER
Lissa Pattillo

EDITOR-IN-CHIEF
Adam Arnold

PUBLISHER
Jason DeAngelis

MY PATHETIC VAMPIRE LIFE VOL. 1
© Ishikawa Rose 2014
All rights reserved.

First published in Japan in 2014 by Futabasha Publishers Ltd., Tokyo.
English version published by Seven Seas Entertainment, LLC.
Under license from Futabasha Publishers Ltd.

No portion of this book may be reproduced or transmitted in any form without written permission from the copyright holders. This is a work of fiction. Names, characters, places, and incidents are the products of the author's imagination or are used fictitiously. Any resemblance to actual events, locals, or persons, living or dead, is entirely coincidental.

Seven Seas books may be purchased in bulk for promotional, educational, or business use. Please contact your local bookseller or the Macmillan Corporate and Premium Sales Department at 1-800-221-7945, extension 5442, or by e-mail at MacmillanSpecialMarkets@macmillan.com.

Seven Seas and the Seven Seas logo are trademarks of
Seven Seas Entertainment, LLC. All rights reserved.

ISBN: 978-1-626923-49-2

Printed in Canada

First Printing: October 2016

10 9 8 7 6 5 4 3 2 1

FOLLOW US ONLINE: ***www.gomanga.com***

READING DIRECTIONS

This book reads from ***right to left***, Japanese style. If this is your first time reading manga, you start reading from the top right panel on each page and take it from there. If you get lost, just follow the numbered diagram here. It may seem backwards at first, but you'll get the hang of it! Have fun!!

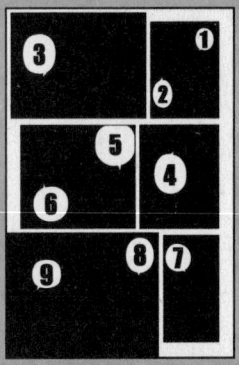

MY PATHETIC
VAMPIRE LIFE

WELL, EVEN IF THE SUN REACHES ME, IT'LL BE A PROBLEM...

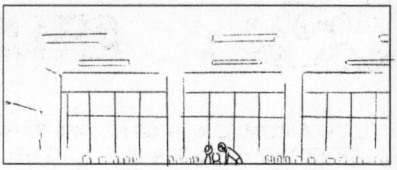

SO, I DREW 5-6 CHAPTERS OF THIS, BUT I COULDN'T SOLIDIFY THE CHARACTERS, THE SETTING, OR THE PLOT.

AND AS YOU CAN SEE, IT WAS BASICALLY UNINTERESTING, SO I DID NUMEROUS DRAFTS, OVER AND OVER.

THIS ISN'T GOING WELL AT ALL, EH--?

FINALLY, WORRIED THAT IT WOULDN'T GO WELL AT ALL, I DEBATED WITH MY FATHER AND RECEIVED THIS MESSAGE FROM MY MOTHER, WHICH I'D LIKE TO QUOTE HERE:

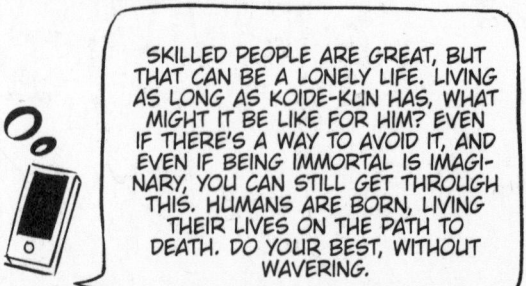

← SHE'S SAYING SOMETHING PROFOUND ABOUT KOIDE.

THANK YOU FOR READING *MY PATHETIC VAMPIRE LIFE* VOLUME 1 ALL THE WAY TO THE END!

AFTERWORD

IT'S A COMMON, FRUSTRATED REFRAIN: FAILING TO CREATE AN EFFECTIVE PERSONA FOR YOURSELF UPON ENTERING SCHOOL, WHERE IDENTITY IS LESS OF A SURE THING AND MORE OF A NECESSITY.

SOMEONE WHO'S GENUINELY CHEERFUL, BUT PLAYS IT COOL. (SOMEONE WHO CHARMS THEIR CLASSMATES. WHO DOESN'T WAIT FOR GOLDEN WEEK TO DO WHAT THEY LIKE.)

SOMEONE WHO'S GLOOMY, BUT TRIES TO BEHAVE LIKE A CHEERFUL TYPE. (THIS IS HELL, BY THE WAY.) IF YOU DO THIS, THE RESULT WILL BE PROFOUND FAILURE, EVERY TIME.

THINK OF IT LIKE THIS: YOU WANT TO GO BACK INTO THE PAST VIA TIME TRAVEL, BUT SINCE TIME TRAVEL IS SCIENTIFICALLY IMPOSSIBLE, YOU HOLD ON TO HOPE FOR THE FUTURE POSSIBILITY OF TIME TRAVEL. BUT THEN IT STILL SEEMS IMPOSSIBLE, SCIENTIFICALLY SPEAKING...

ANYHOW, I TRIED HAVING A VAMPIRE REPEAT HIGH SCHOOL OVER AND OVER.

I KNEW FROM THE START THAT I WANTED TO HAVE A MALE VAMPIRE HIGH SCHOOL STUDENT AS THE MAIN CHARACTER, SO I DREW NUMEROUS DRAFTS FROM THERE.

HERE'S AN EARLY ONE. →

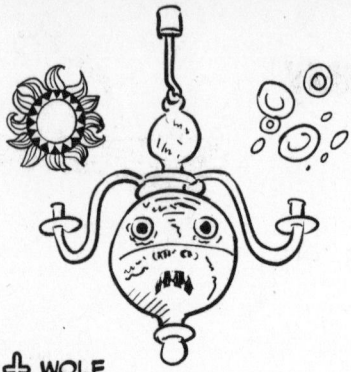

SUN & SANG

THE ENGLISH WORD, "SUN" IS FOR THE SUN ITSELF. THE FRENCH WORD "SANG" MEANS BLOOD AND IS PRONOUNCED THE SAME WAY.

HOMEROOM TEACHER, HAMANO

42 YEARS OLD.
AN UNLUCKY AGE.

WOLF

THE OLD HAIRSTYLE OF THE "YANKEE" TYPES. THEY WOULD GROW THEIR HAIR OUT IN THE BACK. IT'S ALSO CALLED THE JUMBO CUT, NAMED FOR A FAMOUS GOLFER.

IN AMERICA, IT'S REFERRED TO AS A MULLET, NAMED FOR A TYPE OF FISH.

IN AMERICA, IT'S ALSO REFERRED TO AS THE WORLD'S WORST HAIRSTYLE.

SEARCHLIGHTS COMING FROM PACHINKO SHOPS

I'VE RECEIVED INFORMATION THAT NOW EVEN SOME PACHINKO PARLORS (UNCOMMON IN SIZE) HAVE SEARCHLIGHTS ON THE ROOF.

MIYAMA-SENSEI

THE TEACHER IN THE NURSE'S OFFICE. 28 YEARS OLD. LIKES LIGHT NOVELS. FASHIONABLE. INCIDENTALLY, THE P.E. TEACHER'S NAME IS IBUKI.

IBUKI-SENSEI

PHYS. ED TEACHER.
28 YEARS OLD. DARK COMPLEXION. IS A PAIN.

GLOSSARY

SEPTUAGINT HIGH SCHOOL

REFERS TO THE "SEPTUAGINT" (A GREEK TRANSLATION OF THE OLD TESTAMENT). NO SPECIAL MEANING. IT JUST SOUNDED GOOD.

KENCLUCKY

I'VE HEARD MICHAEL JACKSON LOVED IT. THAT ISN'T EXACTLY WHY, BUT I FIGURED VAMPIRES MUST LOVE IT TOO. NO SPECIAL REASON.

FALSE PSYCHIC

I REMEMBER READING A BOOK ABOUT NAPOREONZU (A MAGICIAN) AND HOW HE USED MAGIC TO PERFORM TELEPATHY...

DALI

SALVADOR DALI. HE PAINTED SEVERAL FAMOUS PAINTINGS INCLUDING THE ONE WITH THE MELTING CLOCKS. DALI'S NAME WAS WRITTEN ON MIURA'S CHEEK. NOW, WHICH OF KOIDE'S "BRO" CLASSMATES DID IT IS UNDER DEBATE, BUT ALL AGREE: IT WAS REALLY SURREAL.

MIURA'S 4TH WIFE

A POPULAR BUT STRANGE GIRL IN KOIDE'S CLASS. SHE FELT THAT (WHAT SHE THOUGHT WAS) MIURA'S SENSE OF HUMOR BROUGHT HIM CLOSER TO HER, SO SHE ACCIDENTALLY CONFESSED HER FEELINGS. SHE'S PRETTY DIFFICULT TO USE IN THE STORY, SO THIS WAS HER LAST APPEARANCE.

CHAPTER 8 / END / TO BE CONTINUED...

PSST. COME HERE, YOU GOOD LOOKING GUY...
C'MERE C'MERE.
WHAAA?!
THEN WHAT WAS THE MEEK, PASSIVE ACT ABOUT?

ISN'T HE KIND OF LIKE A MIDDLE-AGED GUY WHO'S SUBMISSIVE AT WORK, THEN ACTS ALL **BIG AND BAD** AT THE BEEF BOWL SHOP?

YOU WERE WORRIED, MIURA MILORD. SO HERE WE ARE, BUT...
YOUR FEARS WERE UN-FOUNDED.
YEAH, BUT HIS BEHAV-IOR...
UH...
WHICH OF THESE SLACKS LOOK BEST ON ME..?

IN THE END, THEY RECOM-MENDED **BLACK CLOTHES**, AND THAT'S WHAT I BOUGHT.

I'M **EMBAR-RASSED** THAT HE'S ONE OF OUR KIND.
YOU'RE RIGHT...

HM? WHAT IS IT?
H-HEY...
SL-SLIDE
BUT THERE'S ONE THING I STILL DON'T UNDERSTAND...
THAT'S WHY I ACTED LIKE THEM.
THAT'S WHY THEY'RE HERE.
ASK THE STORE CLERK.
WHAT KIND OF CLOTHES SHOULD I BUY?
AH. DOES HE NEED HELP?
SWOOP SWOOP
THAT'S TRUE.
.....

HEY, SERIOUSLY... THEY'RE HIGH SCHOOL STUDENTS.
HMM. IF ONLY THERE WASN'T TEXT HERE.
THEY'RE NOT TIMID.
WHERE'S THE MIRROR?
THEY ALWAYS STAND OUT, BUT SEEM SO NATURAL ABOUT IT!
THEY'LL HEM IT FOR FREE?
THE MEDIUM-SIZED CLOTHES HERE...
BROS!
THEY'VE ESTABLISHED THEIR INDIVIDUALITY!

AH, HE'S SHAKING... GUESS HE'S UNCOMFORTABLE HERE AFTER ALL.
I FEEL LIKE I'VE GLIMPSED THE BROS' VERY HEARTS AND SOULS.

WHAT DO YOU THINK OF THIS?
I'M NOT A FAN OF THE COLOR.
OHHH, TURNING DOWN HIS FRIEND'S RECOMMENDATION...! SO WESTERN!

HUH? BUT...
I THOUGHT I WAS THE ONLY ONE WHO WAS ALONE...
...BUT EVERY-ONE'S ON THEIR OWN, AREN'T THEY?

HUH?!

I MISUNDER-STOOD.
I WAS RELYING ON THEM TOO MUCH!

SO... THAT'S HOW IT IS. COULD IT BE?
IS THAT HOW IT IS?

ALL THE BROS ...
...ARE WANDER-ING AROUND ON THEIR OWN.

AND, AREN'T THEY ACTING KIND OF COLD?
HUH? WAS IT DIFFERENT THAN I THOUGHT?

HUH? SOME-THING...? NO, NOTHING.
DID SOME-THING HAPPEN TO YOU?

AH...
SLIDE...
HMM.

PRETEND-ING NOT TO KNOW ME...
MAYBE THEY'RE EMBARRASSED TO THINK OF THEMSELVES AS FRIENDS OF MINE.
...TO IMPRESS THE FASHION-ABLE STORE CLERKS.

HUH ?!
KOFF!

I MEAN, AS OPPOSED TO HOW THEY ARE AT SCHOOL.

THEY ACT NORMAL AT SCHOOL, BUT WOULD THEY SEE ME OUTSIDE AND THINK, "HIM? THAT GUY'S NOT COOL."?
DAMN! SERI-OUSLY?
NO. YOU CAN'T LET THIS GET YOU DOWN...

HM? WHAT'S THE MATTER WITH THAT HIGH SCHOOL STUDENT?
I'M SO BORED... AND LONELY...
UUU... UHUUU...
...AND THOSE BAGS UNDER HIS EYES...IS HE ALL RIGHT? I SHOULD SPEAK TO HIM.
HE LOOKS ILL, THOUGH. REALLY PALE...
EXCUSE ME...
MAYBE HE GOT DISORIENTED, BEING IN A STORE HE WASN'T USED TO?
HE SEEMS KINDA DOWN.
DID THEY FIND SOMETHING THAT SUITS ME?
WH-WHAT'S UP--?
DON'T RUN LIKE THAT IN THE STORE.
HUFF
HUFF
HUFF
HUFF
HUFF
HUFF
OH! MAYBE HE WAS FINE?!
HUH?! WHA?! HUH?! WHA?!
YOOOO, KOIDE!
DASH

CLOTHES THAT WILL FINALLY HELP ME FIT IN!
THERE THEY ARE!
BROS
KOIDE

...A MODERN CLOTHING STORE... (LIKE A TRAVEL PROGRAM ON TV)!
OHHH! THIS MUST BE...

WUH?
WUH?
WUH?
WUH?
WUH?
WUH?
WUH?

OH, RIGHT... I DON'T SHOW UP IN THE MIRROR.

I SHOULD TRY THEM.

I WONDER WHEN I'D WEAR THESE.
SO MANY MAGNIFI-CENT CLOTHES ...

PARCO

CHATTER
ガヤ
CHATTER
ガヤ
CHATTER
ガヤ
CHATTER
ガヤ

THERE...

ALONE...

ALONE...

SUMMER... MEMO-RIES...
WE COULDN'T BUY ANYTHING EXCEPT...
AND THEN (WHETHER WE BUY OUTFITS OR NOT IS IRRELEVANT) THE DRAMA...
IF WE CAN'T GET ANY...
TOOK HOME FREE NEWSPAPERS FROM THE SATURDAY KOSHIEN.
WE GOT 'EM!
WE BOUGHT 'EM!
AWAITS!
IF WE CAN BUY ANY...

CAN'T AFTER SCHOOL COME! ANY SOONER?
I'M REALLY LOOKING FORWARD TO THIS.

HEY! MIND YOUR MANNERS.
THANKS, SENSEI! I'LL DO MY BEST!
OH! EXCUSE MY INTRU-SION.
STAFF ROOM

*Site of Japan's national high school baseball tournament.

↑ 28 YEARS OLD. 150 YEARS OLD. ↑

150 YEARS OLD. ↗ ↖ 223 YEARS OLD.

442 YEARS OLD. 150 YEARS OLD.

THIS IS MY FIRST TIME! MY FIRST!
THE FIRST TIME, SINCE MY BIRTH AND MY DEATH!
I'VE GOTTA TELL SOME-ONE!
I WANNA LOOK AT WALLETS!
WHERE ARE WE GOING?
LEND ME SOME MONEY~!
I CAN'T KEEP SUCH HAPPY FEELINGS BOTTLED UP!
THEY'LL DE-STROY ME FROM THE INSIDE!

YEAH! SHOPPING AFTER SCHOOL! TOTALLY COOL!!
I'LL HAVE TO START LEAVING THE TEXTBOOKS I'D NORMALLY TAKE HOME AT SCHOOL.
I'LL HAVE TO GROW MY HAIR OUT.
AND START WEARING A PARKA UNDER MY SCHOOL UNIFORM.
IF WE WERE GIRLS, WE'D BE GETTING OUR MAKEUP DONE!
AND PUT THIS SEQUENCE OF EVENTS ON YOUTUBE.

FOR A HISTORICAL EXAMPLE...
PARCO
ON THE RUN AFTER BREAKING A STATE TABOO, A CHINESE HIGH PRIEST, ACCOMPANIED BY THREE COMRADES, SET OUT ON AN EXTRAVAGANT ADVENTURE!

AHHH... SO YOU DON'T KNOW HOW?
OH, NOTHING... JUST THAT I'M 150 YEARS OLD, SO OF COURSE I DON'T REALLY LOOK...LIKE A NORMAL HIGH SCHOOL STUDENT.
HUH?
HUH? HUH....?
...YOU'RE COMING WITH US TO BUY SOME CLOTHES!
IN THAT CASE! AFTER SCHOOL, KOIDE...
WHA? HUH?
WHA? HUH? HUH? HUH? WHAAA...?
I WANNA LOOK AT SHOES, TOO.
PARCO, RIGHT?
OH, I WANNA COME! I WAS JUST THINKING ABOUT GOING.

IT STARTED AS A WAY TO HELP US AVOID **STANDING** OUT WHEN WE ATTACKED PEOPLE.
THAT SEEMS TO BE THE SET WARDROBE FOR VAMPIRES, TO WEAR BLACK.

IS YOUR ENTIRE WARDROBE BLACK?
AH, BY THE WAY--WHAT KIND OF CLOTHES DO YOU WEAR **OUTSIDE** OF SCHOOL, KOIDE?

SO HE *DOES* HAVE ALL BLACK!
I MEAN, *I* WEAR BLACK SHIRTS AND PANTS BECAUSE THEY PAIR EASILY WITH OTHER THINGS.

AND THERE AREN'T THAT MANY DARK PLACES ANYMORE.
YEAH... THAT'S TRUE.
IF ANYONE DID THAT NOW, THEY'D BE REALLY CONSPICUOUS.

YEAH, WHY SO DOWN?
WHAT? WHAT IS IT?

Y-YEAH. THAT IS TRUE, BUT...

WELL, YOU COULD TRY BEING **LESS CONSPICUOUS** BY DRESSING LIKE A MODERN-DAY HIGH SCHOOL STUDENT.

THE TIPS OF THOSE SHOES...
IT'S LIKE A BABIRUSA!
※ A breed of pig that inhabits the island of Sulawesi in Indonesia.
HOW DID THEY END UP LIKE THAT?
THAT'S CRAZY.

NO, IT'S BECAUSE THE SHOES DON'T FIT.
IT'S NOT A GOOD FIT FOR A VAMPIRE.

IT JUST HAPPENS TO ANY SHOES I WEAR.
KINDA LIKE PEOPLE WITH CLAW TOES?
ISN'T THAT BECAUSE YOU WALK FUNNY?

YOUR SNEAKERS GET LIKE THAT, TOO?
YEAH...
NO BIGGIE, KOIDE! YOU'RE LIKE A MODEL!

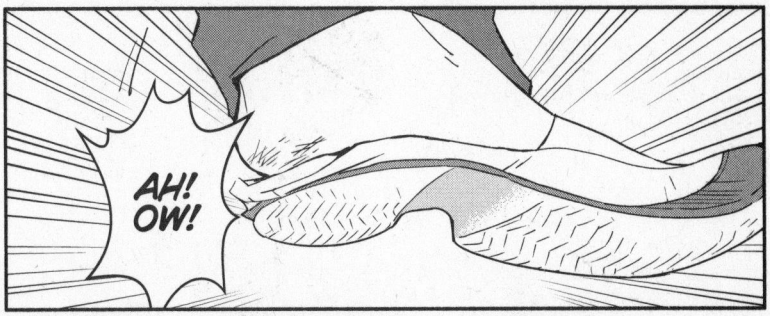
AH! OW!

IT'S TOO SOON FOR THEM TO BE MESSED UP, THOUGH. WE'RE STILL IN THE FIRST SEMESTER.
THAT'S 'CUZ YOU'RE ALWAYS SHUFFLIN' AROUND.
DUDE... I'VE WORN MY INDOOR SHOES DOWN ALREADY.

HMM. YOU TOO, KOIDE?

MY SHOES ARE WORN DOWN, TOO.
AH...IT HAPPENED SO EARLY THIS YEAR.

AH! OWW!
HOW MUCH IS A PAIR OF INDOOR SHOES?
SO, BUY AN-OTHER PAIR.
EH? WHAT'S WRONG, KOIDE?

Chapter 8

4th Week of July
(134th time)

SPEAKING OF NATSUME SOUSEKI...

IT'S WELL-KNOWN THAT, BEGINNING IN 1900, NATSUME SOUSEKI STUDIED ABROAD IN BRITAIN FOR TWO YEARS. BUT APPARENTLY HE SAID THE AIR WAS REALLY BAD IN LONDON, AND FEELING THE AIR POLLUTION WAS SO AWFUL THAT HE AVOIDED THE SUN DURING THE DAY...MAKING HIS EXISTENCE MUCH LIKE A VAMPIRE'S, NO?

AND THEN WE WENT TO KENCLUCKY (FIRST TIME IN A WHILE).

CHAPTER 7 / END

YOU DO LOOK REALLY HAPPY.

HEH. AND IT'S ALL THANKS TO THAT CLASS REP GIRL.
HUH? THAT'S THE FIRST TIME I'VE SEEN THAT FACE ON YOU.

THOUGH, EVERYONE DID SEEM MORE INTERESTED IN ME THAN USUAL.
HUH? N-NO, I DON'T!
I'M TELLING YOU.
I'M TELLING YOU.

ALL RIGHT. I...
HUH? COULD IT BE THAT YOU...?

THAT'S GREAT, KOIDE-KUN!

SIGH...
THE HOMEROOM REP FOR MY CLASS SURE IS **MEDDLESOME.**

I'M A **VAMPIRE,** FOR CRYING OUT LOUD, AND ALL THEIR QUESTIONS WERE COMPLETELY... *ORDINARY.*

I JUST WANTED TO GO HOME EARLY...
...BUT THEN ALL THESE PEOPLE IN MY CLASS...

HEH HEH. BY THE WAY...

SIGH... I GIVE UP.

WHAT ARE MIURA-KUN'S HOBBIES?
WOULDN'T THAT JUST BE READING?
WHAT DOES IT FEEL LIKE, BEING IMMORTAL?
IT'S LIKE A SUNDAY THAT NEVER ENDS.
WHY DID K HAVE TO DIE?
YOU GUYS REALLY LIKE KOKORO, DON'T YOU?
IS MIURA-KUN...
IS MIURA-KUN GOING OUT WITH ANYONE?
WE GO TO KEN-CLUCKY, LIKE, TWICE A WEEK. OTHERWISE, NOTHING IN PARTICULAR.
HOW OLD IS YOUR FRIEND MIURA-KUN?
I THINK HE'S, LIKE, 442.
HEY, ALL THESE QUESTIONS ARE ABOUT MIURA!
KOIDE-KUN, WHAT WOULD HAPPEN IF SOMEONE PUT A STAKE THROUGH YOUR HEART?
IS MIURA-KUN... FOREIGN-BORN?
I THINK HE WAS EUROPEAN BEFORE THEY UNIFIED IT IN ANY WAY.
I WOULD DISAPPEAR, AND...THAT WAS MY TEACHER ASKING THAT.

AND THE QUESTIONS WENT ON UNTIL LONG AFTER SCHOOL WAS OVER...
WHEN WERE YOU BORN?
IN 1864, AROUND THE SAME TIME AS THE AUTHOR NATSUME SOUSEKI.
DO YOU SLEEP AT NIGHT?
I DON'T HAVE TO, BUT ON THE WEEKENDS I SLEEP THROUGH THE DAY.
WHAT DO YOU USUALLY EAT?
KOIDE, ARE YOU "K" FROM HIS WORK, KOKORO?
DO YOU TAKE BATHS?
NO.
I CAN'T USE WATER, BUT BEING DEAD I DON'T REALLY GET DIRTY OR SWEAT, EITHER.
I SAW THE FIRST SINO JAPANESE WAR, I PARTICIPATED AND WAS EVEN DEPLOYED.
WELL, HAVE YOU BEEN IN A WAR?
WHAT DOES IT FEEL LIKE WHEN YOU'RE OUT IN THE SUN?
MY BODY AND MIND ARE SO SICKENED THAT I FEEL HELPLESS, LIKE I WANNA DISAPPEAR.

OVER HERE!
ME, TOO.
OKAY! I HAVE A QUES-TION!

OVER HERE!
I WANNA ASK SOME-THING.

AH... THE CLASS IS...
ME, TOO!

OKA-Y! KOIDE, HOW'S YOUR HOME LIFE?
OH!
ME, TOO...
I SLEEP IN A COFFIN.

...PUTTING KOIDE-KUN AT ITS CENTER... UNITING AROUND HIM.
I HAVE A QUESTION ...!

HM... MHMM...

BUT THERE'S ONE *OTHER* REASON WE HATE TOMATOES.
WAIT FOR IT...
HE'S THE REAL DEAL, ISN'T HE?
HE'S BREAKING THIS DOWN PRETTY WELL.
OHHH... THAT MAKES SENSE.
YEAHHH...

THE WORD "WOLF" BEING IN THERE ALONE IS ENOUGH TO VEX ME...
VAMPIRES DESPISE WOLVES.
AHEM...
THE SCIENTIFIC TERM FOR TOMATO IS "LYCOPERSICUM," WHICH CONTAINS THE GREEK WORD FOR **WOLF**.

IT'S LIKE HE STARTED A CONVERSATION WITH SOMEONE ELSE.
WASN'T HE TALKING DIFFERENT A SECOND AGO?
HEY... DOES IT FEEL LIKE HE GOT SMARTER ALL OF A SUDDEN?

SCRIBBLE
HIS WAY OF LIFE... ISN'T IT SURPRISINGLY INTERESTING?
BUT... IT'S STILL KINDA INTERESTING.
TAKING NOTES

SOMEONE ELSE.

HE'S TALKING LIKE AN EX-SMOKER.
IT MAKES ME THINK OF...IT.
ALSO... PLEASE STOP PUTTING SO MANY BLOOD-SUCKING SCENES IN MOVIES AND ON TV.
...ESPECIALLY HERE IN THE CITY.
THERE AREN'T THAT MANY PLACES TO GET BLOOD ANYMORE...
MAYBE ALL THIS SHARED SPACE ISN'T SO GREAT.
...DO YOU JUST DRINK TOMATO JUICE OR SOMETHING?
HA HA HA!
IS IT? LIKE, NOW, INSTEAD OF BLOOD...
LIKE AN ADDICTION?
SO, IS THAT HOW BLOOD IS FOR VAMPIRES?
DO YOU REALLY THINK VAMPIRES, WHO HATE THE SUN ABOVE ALL ELSE, COULD DRINK THE JUICE OF SUCH A VEGETABLE?
TOMATOES ARE SOMETIMES REFERRED TO AS THE "BLESSING OF THE SUN"...
dono di sole
THERE'S NO WAY A VAMPIRE COULD DRINK TOMATO JUICE.
OH, NO. NO WAY.

YEAH...?
KOIDE-KUN...!

HUH ...?!

HE'S CLEARLY ACTING SUPE-RIOR!
HE'S TALKING... REALLY SLOWLY
I...SEE. BLOOD... RIGHT?
GROWL ...

HAMANO! DON'T ANSWER FOR ME--!
NOT AS MUCH AS THEY USED TO.

...SINCE I LAST DRANK BLOOD.
YEAH, BUT... IT'S BEEN MORE THAN TEN YEARS...

BUT YOU'RE A VAMPIRE.
WHAT? YOU DON'T SUCK BLOOD?

I'M A BIT DISAP-POINTED, FRANKLY.
MUTTER
MUTTER
I CAN'T BELIEVE HIMAWARI-SAN WOULD ASK SOME-THING SO DUMB.
MUTTER
I THOUGHT THE CLASS REP WOULD AT LEAST HAVE ENOUGH SENSE TO AVOID CLICHÉ.
CHITTER
REALLY ...?
CHATTER

JUST HOLD ON A SECOND.

WELL... ACTU-ALLY...

WAAAAAH!!
OH... I'M SO EMBAR-RASSED!

CLATTER
MY DELU-SIONAL LITTLE BROTHER ALSO WANTS TO KNOW...
CLANK
I WAS AFRAID TO ASK, TOO.

I'VE BEEN WANTING TO ASK IF HE SUCKS BLOOD FOR A WHILE NOW... I WAS JUST TOO EMBAR-RASSED TO ASK!
M-ME, TOO...

...THAT'S WHAT I WANTED TO ASK, TOO.
CLATTER

AND ME...
CLANK
CLATTER
CLATTER
ME TOO...
CLANK

IT'S THE MODERATOR HERSELF ...!!

OKAY... HERE WE GO.
SHOOT! I HAVEN'T EVEN THOUGHT OF A QUES-TION...

WHAT KIND OF QUESTION IS SHE GOING TO ASK?
OH WELL... SHE IS THE REPRESEN-TATIVE.
CHATTER
CHATTER
CHATTER

WELL, I GUESS I'M TAKING PART IN MY OWN WORK... HA HA.
HEH. I GOT SO SHOCK-ED, MY OWN HAND WENT UP...

DO YOU... SUCK BLOOD?
UMM... WELL...

IS THE GAP BETWEEN KOIDE-KUN AND THE REST OF THE CLASS EVEN LARGER THAN I THOUGHT?
REALLY? IS NO ONE INTERESTED IN VAMPIRES?
AH... I NEVER EVEN CONSIDERED THAT NO ONE WOULD HAVE QUESTIONS...

IT IS THE FIRST SEMESTER OF HIGH SCHOOL, AFTER ALL.
THEY ARE AT THAT AGE...
OH! I BET THEY'RE EMBARRASSED TO ASK KOIDE QUESTIONS IN FRONT OF EVERYONE LIKE THIS.

SHOOP
WELL... OKAY, THEN.

WHOOOA... THAT BRITISH CAPTAIN WAS AWFUL.
HE LOOKS LIKE HE'S TRYING TO ESCAPE REALITY...
※ HE'S REMEMBERING THE NORMANTON INCIDENT OF 1886.

AHH... SOMEONE, PLEASE, ASK KOIDE-KUN A QUESTION...

※ ONCE VAMPIRES START COUNTING, IT'S REALLY HARD TO STOP.

SIGH... BUT NO MATTER HOW MANY TIMES I TRY, I JUST CAN'T GET USED TO THIS PLACE.
I'VE ALWAYS JUST WANTED TO LIVE AND LET LIVE AS A VAMPIRE...
I'VE NEVER BEEN POPULAR.
SO... NONE, THEN...?
STOP-PPP...!
...AND QUICKLY HEALS US.
...REGEN-ERATION SETS IN...
SHFF...
EVEN IF VAMPIRES GET INJU-RIES OR WOUNDS...
BUT THE WOUNDS ON MY HEART NEVER HEAL!
AAAAGH!

SEE?! THIS IS HOW IT ALWAYS GOES!!

HUH...? ME?
CHATTER
CHITTER
YOU'RE ASKING...
CHATTER
CHATTER
QUES-TIONS... HMM.

EXCEPT... I'M ALREADY DEAD!
I'M SO EMBAR-RASSED I COULD DIE!

UGH. THIS IS LIKE A PUBLIC EXECU-TION.
UM, GUYS? SO... NO ONE HAS A QUESTION FOR KOIDE-KUN?

...TO THE FACT THAT THERE'S NO IN-TEREST.
THERE'S NO NEED TO DRAW ATTEN-TION...

HEY! THAT'S NOT SOMETHING A TEACHER SHOULD SAY.
IT'S LIKE, DON'T TROUBLE YOURSELF ON MY ACCOUNT.
AND SINCE I ALREADY KNOW ALL ABOUT KOIDE, IT'S BORING FOR ME.
SIIIGH...
THIS YEAR, I'LL MAKE THINGS RIGHT!
IT'S OKAY, KOIDE-KUN!
THAT'S... ALSO TRUE.
ALSO, NO ONE EVER GETS EXCITED ABOUT IT.
LET'S BEGIN ASKING KOIDE-KUN SOME QUESTIONS!
WELL, THEN, EVERY-ONE...!
SIIILENCE...
MEETING TO DEEPEN INTERACTION WITH THE DESIRED KOIDE-KUN

HE SUPPORTS ME...
UH...WELL, IT SOUNDS LIKE YOU REALLY WANT TO...
PLEASE?
OUR HOMEROOM TEACHER, HAMANO, ENTHUSIASTICALLY APPROVED THIS MEETING.
GLANCE
BUT... SUCH AN AMAZING MEETING... IS UNPRECEDENTED.
WHA...? THAT'S STRANGE. HE SEEMS EVEN MORE DEJECTED.
WOW... THAT'S A BIG YAWN!
DU-DUUN
HOMEROOM TEACHER HAMANO (FIRST APPEARANCE)
RIGHT, KOIDE? WE DID THIS LAST YEAR, TOO?
YUP.
WELL... WE DO SOMETHING LIKE THIS EVERY YEAR.
WHAT? THIS ISN'T GROUND-BREAKING ENOUGH FOR YOU?!
HEY, HAMANO-SENSEI! WHAT'S WITH THE BORED ATTITUDE?!

MEETING TO DEEPEN INTERACTION WITH THE DEJ ED KOIDE-KUN
パチ CLAP
パチ CLAP
パチ CLAP
パチ CLAP
パチ CLAP
HOW'S THIS, KOIDE-KUN?
NOW YOU CAN GET CLOSER TO EVERY-ONE!
GLANCE
FIGURES SHE'D DO SOMETHING SO POINT-LESS.

Chapter 7
3rd Week of July, part 2 (134th time)
MEETING TO DEEPEN INTERACTION WITH THE DEJECTED KOIDE-KUN
HUH? WHAT'S WITH THIS "MEETING TO DEEPEN INTERACTION"?
WHO KNOWS.
WHAT IS SHE DOING?
CHATTER
CHITTER
CHATTER
CHATTER
UH, HEY, EVERYONE! TODAY, FOR HOMEROOM...
...I'D LIKE YOU ALL TO CONSIDER... VAMPIRES.
OUR FIRST SEMESTER IS ALMOST OVER...
...BUT EVEN THOUGH WE HAVE A VAMPIRE AMONG US, THERE'S SO MUCH WE DON'T KNOW ABOUT HIM!
SO, I THOUGHT I'D CREATE AN OPPORTUNITY FOR US TO ASK KOIDE-KUN QUESTIONS...
...TO HELP US DEEPEN OUR UNDERSTANDING OF VAMPIRES.

THAT WAS HIMAWARI-SAN, OUR CLASS REP.
SIGH...
SHE'S SO SMART, AND GETS THINGS DONE! I REALLY ADMIRE HER!

HIMAWARI-SAN LOOKED REALLY SURPRISED AND RAN OUT OF THE CLASSROOM JUST NOW.
CHATTER
I BET SHE WAS HEADED FOR THE STAFF ROOM.
CHATTER
BUT SHE DID IT MORE LIKE A PROPER BRISK WALK.
CHATTER
THAT'S OUR CLASS REP, ALL RIGHT!
CHATTER

...I'VE GOT A BAD FEELING ABOUT THIS.

UGH...
FOR SOME REASON...

1-1

HIS HEART IS COLD AND CUT OFF FROM THE WORLD!
AGH... AND IT WENT JUST AS I THOUGHT IT WOULD!

HE'S ALWAYS ALONE. I GOT WORRIED, SO I TRIED TO TALK TO HIM...
KOIDE-KUN!...

IT'S MY DUTY, AS CLASS REPRESEN-TATIVE!
I'VE GOT TO WARM HIM UP!

WHO WAS THAT...?

I'LL SAVE YOU!
HANG ON, KOIDE-KUN!
DASH

JUST BECAUSE YOU'RE DEAD DOESN'T MEAN YOUR LIFE IS OVER!
WHIP

BUT ONE OF THEM IS SOMETHING YOU **LOVE**, AND THE OTHER IS SOMETHING YOU **HATE**. WHAT DO YOU THINK? ***INTERESTING***, RIGHT?
HEY, KOIDE-KUN! SO, IN ENGLISH, "SUN" REFERS TO THE **SUN** IN THE SKY, RIGHT? AND IN FRENCH, THE WORD "SANG" MEANS **BLOOD**. THE SPELLING IS DIFFERENT, BUT BOTH WORDS' JAPANESE PRONUNCIATION, "SAN," IS SIMILAR...

HE WON'T EVEN **LOOK** AT ME!
HE'S IGNORING ME!

SHE JUST KEEPS GOING.

My Pathetic Vampire Life

A DAY IN THE LIFE OF RUI-KUN

I... ALSO WANT TO PET THEM...

EVEN THOUGH THAT JUST MAKES US HURT MORE.
...BUT AT LEAST HE'S TRYING TO HELP US ENJOY OURSELVES.
RUI-KUN MAY BE BORING...

...BUT SINCE I CAN'T, I JUST PAT MYSELF ON THE BACK, FOR DOING THE RIGHT THING.
?!
?!
?!
GUAK
GUA
AK

HEY! YOU BETTER NOT EAT THEM!
RUMMBLE
OUR TEACHER IS PRETTY DUMB.
CHAPTER 6 / END

AH...
THEY'RE LOOKING SO INTENTLY AT THE ANMALS...
WAIT. DOES THAT MEAN THEY'RE ...?!

FLAP
AND I WANNA PET THEM!
FLAP
RUI-KUNNN, THIS IS BORRI-INNG...
AHH
THIS IS SO HARD!
AWW
AWW
AWW
AWW
GUAK
GUAK

I WANT TO PET IT...
BUT THAT RABBIT... IS SO CUTE.

ANIMALS THIS SMALL WOULD DIE INSTANTLY!
FLAP
SHAKE
SHAKE
GUAA!
AH, NO, YOU CAN'T! THAT'LL SHORTEN ITS LIFESPAN!
GWAAK
FLAP
SLAP
FLAP
SHAKE
SHAKE

I WANTED TO PET IT, TOO.
.....

THAT'S TRUE...

RABBIT POOP

NAH, THAT'S JUST THE DUCKS' FEATHERS FLYING AROUND DUE TO THE STRESS.
BUT RUI-KUN LOOKS SO HAPPY.
DOESN'T HE LOOK LIKE AN ANGEL?
IT'S SO IRONIC.
RUI-KUN'S SUCH A NICE GUY...
BOING
GAAH! QUACK
RUI-KUN... THAT'S TOO PITIFUL.
TREMBLE
TREMBLE
SHAKE
SHAKE

QUAAAAAUK!
QUAACK
HOP HOP HOP
QUAACK
QUAACK
RUSTLE RUSTLE
WAA!
QUAACK
RUSTLE RUSTLE
THE ANIMALS ARE SCARED TO DEATH OF HIM.
IT CAN'T BE HELPED. A CREATURE FROM THE TOP OF THE FOOD CHAIN JUST WALKED IN.
HE MAY AS WELL BE A LION.

ギャア
QUAAACK
FLOP
FLOP
BONK
BONK
ガシャン
ガシャン
ギャアア
QUACK
CLATTER
ガシャン
CRASH
ガシャン
ギャ
QUAACK

SEE?
QUAACK
AREN'T THEY CUTE?
QUACK QUACK
OP OP OP
HOP
YEAH...

WELL, THEN... TIME TO CLEAN!

UH, THIS IS THE THIRD FLOOR.
OKAY! LET'S GO, RUI-KUN!
STOMP
OKAY!
OKAY... THAT'S FINE...
HOW 'BOUT YOU, MIURA ?!
I-I'M IN! I'M GOING!
ALL RIGHT... I'LL JUST CLOSE UP THE GYM AND HEAD HOME, THEN.
THIS WAY.
WHICH WAY? WHICH WAY?
UM-BRELLAS, YOU TWO. UMBREL-LAS.
FWOO
DASH
DASH
JEEZ, THEY JUMPED DOWN IN THEIR INDOOR SHOES.
HEY, ANIMALS! YOU DOING ALL RIGHT?

TO THE ANIMAL HUTCH. NO MATTER WHAT'S GOING ON IT SHOULDN'T MATTER ONCE YOU SEE THOSE LITTLE ANIMALS.
KOIDE-KUN, YOU COMING TOO?
HUH? WHERE?

SMALL... ANIMALS ...?
HUH?

THEY WON'T BITE?
THEY WON'T! AND YOU CAN'T BITE THEM EITHER, KOIDE-KUN!
IT'S FINE. I WON'T EAT THEM.
TH-THERE AREN'T ANY DOGS OR ANY-THING IN THERE?
NOTHING BUT RABBITS AND DUCKS!
ARE THEY CUTE?
OF COURSE THEY'RE CUTE!

THEY MOVE ON...AND FORGET ABOUT US.
THEY FORGET ABOUT US SO SOON, YOU KNOW?

AND ON TOP OF FORGET-TING ABOUT US...
...THEY DIE BEFORE WE DO.

BOONG
BOONG

OH! I HAVE TO GO CLEAN OUT THE ANIMAL PEN.

WE HAVE TO ACCEPT THE COST OF BEING IMMORTAL.
IT'S ALL RIGHT.

...BUT I'LL BE IN 12TH GRADE AGAIN NEXT YEAR TOO, SO I CAN'T GO ON TO COLLEGE.
EVERYONE IN THE 12TH GRADE IS WORRIED ABOUT ENTRANCE EXAMS...
...SO MY CLASS-MATES CAN FOCUS ON THEIR STUDIES.
EVEN SO, I WANT TO HELP OUT HOWEVER I CAN!...
I'M TRYING TO DO ALL OF THE STUFF OUTSIDE OF STUDYING.
AND THE ANIMAL CARE COMMITTEE, THE BEAUTIFICATION COMMITTEE, THE HEALTH COMMITTEE, THE CLEANING COMMITTEE, PLUS I'M A GRADE-LEVEL REPRESENTATIVE AND AN EXECUTIVE MEMBER OF THE CULTURE FESTIVAL COMMITTEE!
THAT'S TOO MUCH.
HE'S LIKE THE ASSISTANT DIRECTOR ON A MOVIE.
THESE HUMANS ...
NO, RUI-KUN, YOU CAN'T LET YOUR-SELF BE USED LIKE THAT!
YOU'VE MAINTAINED AN 'A' IN GYM, EVEN THOUGH YOU HAVEN'T SHOWN UP ONCE.
YOU'RE A GOOD GUY.
DID SOME-THING HAPPEN TO HIM TODAY...?
THEY USE US UP AND TOSS US ASIDE, LIKE TISSUES FROM A BOX.
THAT'S SO UNFUNNY, IT'S SAD.
YOU SHOULD GET AN 'E'...FOR BEING AN EXCELLENT GUY.

BUT YOU'RE MUCH OLDER THAN I AM.
BY OVER 200 YEARS.
BUT, RUI-KUN, YOU BECAME A VAMPIRE WHEN YOU WERE EIGHTEEN.

AND, MUELLER-SAN, YOU SEEM TO BE ON THE PATH TO **ADULT-HOOD.**
PLEASE STOP ADDING "SAN."
AND STOP CALLING ME BY MY TRUE NAME.

OH, RUI, BY THE WAY... WHAT HAVE YOU BEEN DOING UP TO NOW?

AND I BECAME ONE AT SIXTEEN.
WHY, YOU'RE A YOUNG'UN, THEN.
THOSE TWO ARE A MESS.
THEIR ACTUAL AGES ARE **SO DIFFER-ENT** FROM HOW THEY LOOK AND ACT.

YOU'RE ALWAYS SO IMPRES-SIVE, RUI.
WELL, I **AM** ON THE MAIN-TENANCE COMMITTEE!

OH! THE GLASS ON THE THIRD FLOOR BROKE...
...SO I WAS CLEANING AND REPAIRING IT.

RUI KEIJU
18 years old
(205th time)
A VAMPIRE IN 12TH GRADE AT THIS SCHOOL.
HE'S AS FRIENDLY AS HE LOOKS.

KOIDE-KUN... HAVE YOU GOTTEN TALLER?
NO. I STOPPED GROWING.

AH. ONE OF MY OWN KIND AND IBUKI-SENSEI.
OH! WELL, I AM A PHYS-ED TEACHER, AFTER ALL.
THAT'S QUITE A SUNTAN, SIR.

BUT YOU SEEM TO BE LIVING A HEALTHY LIFESTYLE.
I'M DEAD.
RUI-KUN IS NOT VERY FUNNY.

ALWAYS SO BRIGHT AND LOUD AT NIGHT...
THEY HAD SEARCH-LIGHTS COMING FROM THE PACHINKO PARLORS.
THAT MUST'VE BEEN QUITE A SIGHT.

THAT'S WHY I HATED THE '80s.
MIURA, YOU CAN'T TAKE THAT MUCH FUSS, CAN YOU?
I SEEEE...

OH! RUI-KUN!

HEY! ON YOUR WAY HOME?

THERE WAS A TIME WHEN THE GLASS USED TO GET BROKEN ALL THE TIME, WHEN WAS IT?
HUH? I DON'T KNOW.
WHEN WAS IT, MIURA?
SOME-TIME IN THE '80s. IT WAS ANNOY-ING.
AH, THAT'S RIGHT. IT WAS WHEN THERE WERE ALL THOSE DELIN-QUENTS.
THAT'S AROUND THE TIME I WAS BORN, SO THERE'S NO WAY I'D KNOW.
THE TYPES THEY CALLED "YANKEE" USED TO GROW THEIR HAIR OUT IN THE BACK, RIGHT?
WHAT WAS THAT HAIRSTYLE CALLED?
IT WAS CALLED "THE WOLF," RIGHT?
ISN'T THAT AWFUL?
OH, RIGHT. YOU GUYS HATE WOLVES, DON'T YOU?
SPEAKING OF WHICH, YOU GUYS KEEP YOUR HAIR SHORT, RIGHT?
ANYWAY... THAT WAS AN AWFUL PERIOD IN TIME.
I HAVE NO INTEREST IN RE-VISITING IT.

ミーン
ミーン
ミーン
ミーン
THERE WAS A TIME WHEN THE WINDOWS WERE ALWAYS BROKEN...
HOW LONG AGO WAS IT?
.....
WHAT YEAR WAS IT?
I'D BETTER NOT TOUCH HIM...
CHICKA CHICKA CHIRP
オーシン
ツツ
オーシン

THEY'RE LIVING FOR THE HERE AND NOW.
UGH... IT FIGURES THAT THESE BROS CAN'T THINK THAT FAR AHEAD.

OOH!

HEY! THE GLASS ON THE THIRD FLOOR IS BROKEN!
NO WAY, REALLY ?!
LET'S GO SEE!
RATTLE
RATTLE

SPEAKING OF WHICH...

AAH!
SIGH...

AND YOU DO KNOW IF YOU HOLD ON TO A DEAD PERSON FOR TOO LONG YOUR OWN LIFE WILL SHORTEN, RIGHT?
SERI-OUSLY ?!
CLATTER

IT'S SIMPLY THE LAW OF NATURE. LIKE WHEN AIR MOVES FROM A WARM PLACE TO A COLD PLACE...
...EXCEPT THAT IT FLOWS FROM A PLACE WHERE THERE IS LIFE, TO ANOTHER WHERE THERE'S NONE.

YOU'RE GONNA SUCK MY BLOOD ?!
I KNEW IT!
NO, NO... IT'S NOT MY CHOICE.

AHA HA HA!
AH... THEY COULD NOT CARE LESS.
THUMP

TO DIE YOUNG... BEFORE HIS TIME...
AND HE'S GONNA GO BALD YOUNG!
BALD-NESS HAS NOTHING TO DO WITH THIS.

I SEEEE... SO I JUST SHORT-ENED MY LIFESPAN.
WUH-OH! YOU'RE GONNA DIE YOUNG!

NO WAY. I WON'T HAND HIM OVER.
WHA--?! LET ME TRY.
MUTTER
MUTTER
MUTTER
WHA--?

IT'S KINDA LIKE WHEN YOU FIRST TOUCH A LIZARD. AT FIRST IT FEELS GROSS, BUT THEN WHEN YOU GET USED TO IT, IT'S MORE LIKE ONE OF THOSE COOLING GEL PADS...NO...MORE LIKE A FAR BETTER SUBSTITUTE.
HMM... WHEN I TOUCH KOIDE, I DO GET CHILLS FOR A SECOND.

SO, FIVE.
AND ONE IN THE 11TH GRADE... AND... TWO IN THE 12TH GRADE.

HMM... WELL, THERE'S MIURA...
KOIDE, JUST HOW MANY VAMPIRES ARE AT THIS SCHOOL?

SO YOU GUYS GO SEE THEM.
SO THERE'S FOUR MORE.
POINT

HEY, WHAT ABOUT...
WHA--?! NO WAY! VAMPIRES ARE SO SCARY!

RIGHT! BECAUSE YOU'RE DEAD!
BECAUSE I'M DEAD.

ミーン
ミーン
ミーン

IT'S SO HOT. I'M JUST WORN DOWN.
CHATTER ガヤ
SUMMER'S TOO LONG.
IT IS HOT...
FLOP FLOP
CHATTER ガヤ
AHHHH... IT'S HOT.

WELL, KOIDE'S COLD, SO IT FEELS GOOD.
AND WHAT ARE YOU DOING?!

Chapter 6
3rd Week of July
(134th time)

CONFUCIUS SAID...
WHEN I WAS 150, I THREW MYSELF INTO MY STUDIES.
AT 300, I STOOD ON MY OWN.
AT 400, I WAS NO LONGER LOST.
AT 500, I LEARNED MY DIVINE PURPOSE.
AT 600, I COULD COMPREHEND ANYTHING I WAS TOLD.
AND AT 700, I COULD FOLLOW MY OWN HEART WITHOUT RUNNING AFOUL OF THE WORLD.
THAT'S NOT WHAT CONFUCIUS SAID.
MY PATHETIC VAMPIRE LIFE

JUST LIKE THE RIVAL OF A FLEDGLING SHOUNEN SERIES HERO.
FWUMP
JUST LIKE THE FLEDGLING HERO OF A SHOUNEN SERIES.

CHAPTER 5 / END

I'M JUST GETTING A LITTLE TIRED OF LIVING FOREVER.

I'M SORRY, MIURA...

SORRY FOR WHAT?
OH...FOR MENTIONING BEING DEAD.

I'VE HAD PLENTY OF TIMES WHERE I GOT FED UP OR FELL INTO DESPAIR.
BUT I'VE BEEN DOING MUCH BETTER FOR THE PAST 150 YEARS, THANKS TO YOU.

...SAY, MIURA-KUN
SLIDE SLIDE
HM? WHAT IS IT, KOIDE-KUN...?

MIURA ...
BLINK BLINK

.....
SOMEHOW IT JUST DOESN'T SEEM TO BOTHER ME ANYMORE.

YEAH! TONIGHT'S SUCH AN ESPECIALLY CLEAR NIGHT.
IT MAKES ME WANT TO DO RADIO CALIS-THENICS!

WHEN NIGHTTIME COMES, I ALWAYS CHEER UP.
IT'S AS IF I SLEPT OFF ALL MY CARES.
RIGHT?
MY SKIN EVEN GETS SHINY!

WHEN YOU HIT FOUR HUNDRED, YOU NO LONGER FEEL LOST.
IS THAT LIKE, "IF YOU MAKE IT TO FORTY, YOU'RE DOING ALL RIGHT"?
THOUGH, I DO GET LOST A LOT...
SIGH...
SEE? THE SUN'S FINALLY GOING DOWN.
JUST NOT TODAY.
IT'LL GET BETTER SOON.
ANYWAY, THE SUN'S STILL OUT IN THE EARLY EVENING. THOSE RAYS CAN GET YOU DOWN.
I DON'T MIND GETTING DOWN.
IT'S BASICALLY LIKE BEING DEAD.

SIGH... TODAY WAS PRETTY HARSH.

WHAT'S UP WITH LIVING FOREVER, ANYWAY?
THAT'S... QUITE PROFOUND.

THAT'S ADOLES-CENCE FOR VAMPIRES.
IS THAT SO?

HEY, HOW OLD ARE YOU AGAIN?
ONE HUNDRED AND FIFTY YEARS OLD.

MIURA...
WHAT'S IT LIKE, HAVING LIVED MORE THAN 400 YEARS?
DO YOU WORRY ABOUT A LOT OF THINGS NOW?
ME? I DON'T REALLY WORRY ANY-MORE.

BEING SIXTEEN FOR THE REST OF MY LIFE WOULD BE *TERRIBLE*, WOULDN'T IT?

SOMEONE WHO IS SIXTEEN FOR ALL ETERNITY

HEY, I SAID QUIT IT!
HOO ワイ
WOO ワイ
CHITTER カ" ャ
CHATTER カ" ャ
KYA HA HA!
SERIOUSLY ?

HEY, BY THE WAY... TSUKINAMI-SAN...
DO HUMANS WISH THEY COULD BE ETERNALLY YOUNG?

HMM... IN THAT CASE, IT'D PROBABLY BE BETTER FOR ME TO BECOME AN ADULT FIRST, RIGHT?
I'D LIKE MY BREASTS TO BE A BIT BIGGER, TOO.

THE MOMENT YOU BECOME A VAMPIRE, YOU COMPLETELY STOP AGING.

YOU MEAN BE-COMING A VAMPIRE?
YOU **STOP AGING** IF YOU BECOME A VAMPIRE, RIGHT?
YEAH.

WEREN'T YOU RESTING IN THE NURSE'S OFFICE?
WHY ARE YOU EVEN MORE TIRED NOW?
YEAH...I THOUGHT I'D GET SOME REST THERE.

THAT TEACHER IN THE NURSE'S OFFICE IS PRETTY COOL, ISN'T HE?
THAT'S WHAT EVERYONE SAYS, ANYWAY.
YEAH... I GUESS HE IS... FOR A HUMAN.

AH! I GET IT NOW!
YOU GOT NERVOUS BECAUSE HE WAS SO COOL, SO YOU COULDN'T REST!

HOW ABOUT ME, THEN? HOW DO VAMPIRES SEE ME?!
COMPLETELY AVERAGE.

THAT'S NOT IT.
WE VAMPIRES HAVE OUR OWN SENSE OF AESTHETIC.

HUH ...?
VAMPIRE SENSE OF AESTHE-TIC...

HE SAYS, "NO WAY."
SERI-OUSLY?! DID YOU EVEN ASK HIM?!
NURSE'S OFFICE
I REALLY DID.
THEN ASK HIM AGAIN!
THIS IS A REAL PAIN...
UM... HE'S SAYING YOUR MANNER OF SPEAKING IS TICKING HIM OFF...FOOL.
THAT MUST BE A LIE! THOSE ARE YOUR WORDS!
SIGH...
CHITTER
CHATTER
CHITTER
CHATTER

THE TEACHER IN THE NURSE'S OFFICE...
SEPTEMBER 9TH
...IS ASKING ME TO BITE HIM.
NO WAY.

...THOSE AREN'T THE EYES OF KILLER, ARE THEY?
OH... A LONG TIME AGO, HE PROBABLY DID KILL A LOT OF PEOPLE.
SOMETIMES HE MAKES THIS FACE.

WELL THEN, HOW ABOUT I TRY AND ASK FOR YOU?
OKAY. ONCE YOU'VE ASKED, COME BY AGAIN.
SQUEEEK

JUST WAIT A MOMENT.

NO PROBLEM. I'M ASKING HIM NOW THROUGH TELEPATHY.
OH, THAT'S CONVE-NIENT.

BITING HUMANS MEANS RISKING AN INCREASE IN THE NUMBER OF MY KIND...
WITHOUT PERMISSION FROM THE TOP, THAT'S A NO-GO.
BUT... WHY NOT?
IT'S JUST A LITTLE BITE.
I DON'T KNOW WHY. I'M WAY AT THE BOTTOM OF THIS CHAIN.
AHHH... WHY NOT ASK MIURA?
HE'S MUCH OLDER THAN I AM.
PAUSE
HUH?
BA-BUMP
IT... IT'S FINE...
SINCE HE'S... REALLY COOL FOR A STUDENT. FOR HIM TO LOOK AT ME WITH THOSE EYES...

YOU CAN'T GO OUT IN THE SUN.
THIS, IN ITSELF, IS A COUNTER-MEASURE AGAINST UV RADIATION! I'M READY!

I MEAN... BEING A VAMPIRE IS PRETTY INCON-VENIENT, YOU KNOW?
THAT'S FINE! I CAN DEAL WITH THAT!

YOUR FACE'LL GET REALLY PALE.
I PREFER PALLOR! I'D GIVE ANY-THING FOR IT!

IF YOU EAT GARLIC, YOUR MOUTH'LL REEK.
HM... IT'S THE SAME FOR HUMANS, THOUGH.

WELL, I CAN SEE YOUR MIND IS MADE UP...AND YOU'VE DONE A LOT FOR ME...
BUT I'M AFRAID IT'S IMPOSSIBLE.
WHAT?! WHAT ARE YOU SAYING?!

WH-WHY?

BITE ME.

SIGH... I GET SO DRIED OUT IN SUMMER.
I'M TERRIFIED OF GETTING WRINKLES.

YES, THE UV RAYS!
THOSE RAYS THAT WREAK HAVOC ON US MALES WITH BEAUTIFUL SKIN!
DA-DAN!!!

THE HARUHI GENERATION IS ALREADY AROUND THIRTY...
THINKING BACK ON IT, I TOO HAVE WISHED WE HAD ALIENS AND ESPERS AT OUR SCHOOL...
AS IF THAT COULD HAPPEN ...
THIS GUY IS REALLY OBNOXIOUS.

SPEAKING OF WHICH.
KOIDE-KUN...

BUT...!
THERE ARE VAMPIRES.

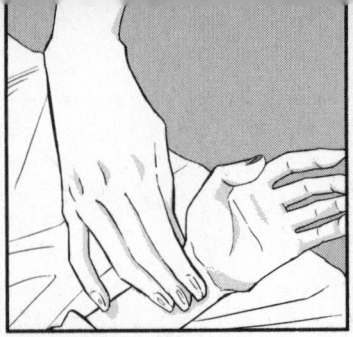

COULD YOU PLEASE SETTLE DOWN? I'M GOING TO HAVE A LOOK AT YOU NOW.
.....

THAT'S WHAT HE WANTED TO SAY.

HE'S... DEAD!
WHAT?! THIS KID...

THE SUN'S RAYS CAN BE ROUGH ON YOU.

OH, I KNOW...
I JUST PASSED OUT FROM MORE-THAN-HEAT-STROKE...
COULD YOU PLEASE... GO EASY ON ME?

ALL... LEADING TO THIS.

I AM A VAMPIRE ...
RESTING IN THE NURSE'S OFFICE.

YOU CAUSED A LOT OF TROUBLE TODAY, GETTING CAUGHT IN THE SUN.
TMP
YOU'RE A VAMPIRE. YOU SHOULD KNOW BETTER.
TMP
I AM A VAMPIRE! THAT'S WHY I'M HERE!
I CAN'T REST.

Chapter 5

2nd Week of July
(134th time)

WELL...I THOUGHT I COULD MAKE IT...
...BUT I COULDN'T... REACH THE OTHER SIDE.
SPEAKING OF WHICH, I SEE A LOT OF DRIED-UP EARTHWORMS WHEN I'M WALKING AROUND THIS TIME OF YEAR...
THEIR SPIRITS ARE COM-PLETELY BROKEN.

YOU LOOK JUST LIKE THEM.
I DON'T THINK SO!
YOU'VE BEEN ALIVE 150 YEARS, AND YOU DON'T KNOW?

SHEESH... FOR AN IMMORTAL, YOU SURE ARE A HANDFUL.
GLANCE
AT ANY RATE, LET'S GET YOU TO NURSE'S OFFICE.
MIIIN
MIN MIN
MIIIN

KOIDE GOT CAUGHT IN THE SUN AGAIN!
NOT GOOD!

DIDN'T WE TELL YOU NOT TO USE THE WALK-WAY WHEN GOING TO THE OTHER BUILDING?
THAT ONE DOESN'T HAVE A ROOF.
IT MIGHT BE THE LONG WAY, BUT GO THROUGH THE FIRST FLOOR NEXT TIME.
YOU'RE JUST BEING LAZY, AREN'T YOU...

MY PATHETIC VAMPIRE LIFE

BATS

THE LATIN TERM FOR BAT IS **CHIROPTERA.**

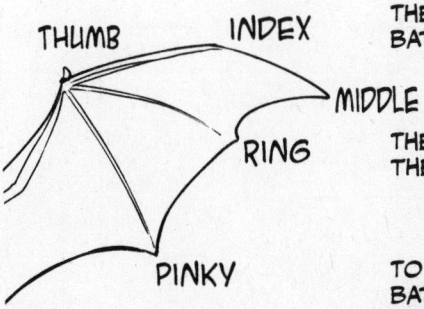

THE TWO PARTS OF THE WORD:
CHIRO IS HAND.
PTERA IS WING.

TO PUT IT MORE SIMPLY, BATS HAVE HANDS WITH HUGE PALMS ATTACHED TO THEIR WINGS...

THERE'S A MEMBRANE ATTACHED TO THE SIDE OF THEIR BODIES.

PERHAPS THAT'S WHY, LONG AGO, THE SIDES OF VESTS WORN BY VAMPIRES WERE LACED UP...

...SO THAT WHEN THE VAMPIRES TRANSFORMED INTO BATS, THEY WOULDN'T RIP THE SIDES OF THEIR VESTS.

THAT'S THE STORY, ANYWAY.

A DAY IN THE LIFE OF MIURA

CHAPTER 4 / END

KI
KI
SQUAWK
SQUAWK
SQUAWK
GRRRR!
ONCE UPON A TIME, THERE WAS A GROUP OF BIRDS AND A GROUP OF BEASTS IN CONFLICT.
A BAT FLEW OVERHEAD, OBSERVING THE STATE OF THINGS.
FLAP
FLAP
FLAP
FLAP
WHEN THE BIRD GROUP GAINED THE UPPER HAND...
...THE BAT SAID, "SINCE I HAVE WINGS, I'M THE BIRDS' ALLY."
AND WHEN THE BEASTS GAINED THE ADVANTAGE...
BUT REALLY, I'M A MAMMAL.
NO, REALLY. I AM
...THE BAT SAID, "I'M LIKE A MOUSE AND I HAVE FANGS, SO I'M A BEAST."
FLAP
FLAP
FLAP
FLAP
HE CONTINUED TO FLAP BACK AND FORTH...

EXCEPT NOT ME?
DAMN... MAYBE SHE JUST HAS A THING FOR UNDER-DOGS?

SHALL WE GO?
I HAVE NO IDEA. I'M TOTALLY FLUM-MOXED.
IS IT THE FORBID-DEN FRUIT ASPECT?!
IS IT THAT *TWI-LIGHT* BOOK ?!
AREN'T YOU MORE THAN SATISFIED WITH YOUR HIGH SCHOOL LIFE?!
DAMN! WHAT'S SO **AT-TRACTIVE** ABOUT YOU, ANYWAY?!

I THINK BEING A BAT WOULD DEFINITELY SUIT YOU.
YEEAH...

I WONDER IF I COULDN'T TRANS-FORM INTO A BAT, TOO...!
HMPH.

YEAH... THERE WAS AN AESOP'S FABLE THAT WENT LIKE THIS...

HUH? WHY?

UM, IF YOU DON'T MIND, COULD WE BE FRIE... NO, YOUR THIRD... OR EVEN FOURTH! PLEASE MAKE ME YOUR FOURTH WIFE!
FOR-EVER MORE!
FOR-EVER...?
BOW
UH, THAT'S FINE, BUT...
.....
LOOKS LIKE I MADE A FEMALE FRIEND.
I...DON'T REALLY GET HOW, THOUGH.
KYAA!
KYAA!
ALL I WANT IS TO CON-TINUE MY PEACEFUL, QUIET LIFE, ALONE...
HEY! AT LEAST YOU CAN SAY THAT!

↑ IT'S THE SCENT OF DEATH.

BUT THIS TIME THINGS WILL WORK OUT!
IT HASN'T BEEN FINE WITH YOU UP TO THIS POINT, HAS IT?
THAT'S FINE THOUGH, ISN'T IT?
I WAS NEVER INTERESTED IN TAKING FULL ADVANTAGE OF HIGH SCHOOL, LIKE YOU ARE.
RUB
RUB
RUB
RUB
UM... MIURA-KUN?
WELL, ANYHOW... I'LL JUST CONTINUE ON MY PEACEFUL WAY.
SHAKE
TREMBLE
TREMBLE
SHAKE
THIS GIRL... OVER HERE...
HUH? ME?
MIURA-KUN? COULD YOU COME HERE FOR A SECOND?
THAT GIRL'S FROM MY CLASS.

THERE WAS A LOT OF CHATTER IN THE CLASSROOM.
CHATTER...

I MAY BE MORE THAN 400 YEARS OLD, BUT IT'S STILL A SORE SPOT FOR ME.
SO TO BE THOUGHT OF AS NOT SO INTRIGUING IS...QUITE VEXING.
I'M PASSIVE, BUT I HAVE A CERTAIN AIR OF MYSTERY...

SO I JUST WANTED A PEACEFUL, UNEXCITING LIFE...I THOUGHT BEING AVERAGE WOULD BE ENOUGH.
JUST BEING AROUND FOR 400 YEARS MEANS I'VE ACCRUED MANY SINS...

.....
IT'S SO WEIRD...

SO? ARE YOU IN A HIGHER CASTE NOW?
NO.
CAN'T YOU TELL?
HE GOT DOODLED ON, TOO.

WELL, IF IT MAKES YOU HAPPY...
I'LL BECOME A BAT, OR WHATEVER IT TAKES.

MY MORNING CLASSES WENT ON LIKE NORMAL...
BUT BY EARLY AFTERNOON, I SUDDENLY HAD ALL THIS ON MY FACE.

MIURA...

SPEAKING OF WHICH... THIS IS REALLY BAD.
SO IN CLASS, I'M THE QUIET, PASSIVE TYPE.

I AM SO, SO SORRY!

THEY DID THIS TO ME.

Face doodles: SALV DALI.

DON'T DOODLE ON HIS FACE!
LET'S DRAW HIM A GOATEE
AND SOME GLASSES
YEAH! IT SHOULD BE CUTER!
THIS BAT'S STARTING TO PISS ME OFF!
...THIS IS PRETTY MUCH MY SCHOOL LIFE.
CHATTER
CHATTER
CHATTER
SINCE VAMPIRES ARE FEEBLE DURING THE DAY...
ALSO...
BUH-BYE!
LATER!
HE'S IN THE SAME GRADE AS ME, BUT HE'S LIVED LONGER AND AMASSED MUCH MORE KARMA.
...THERE'S ANOTHER VAMPIRE IN THE NEXT CLASS OVER.

WELL, RIGHT NOW WE'RE COMMUNICATING VIA ULTRASONIC WAVES.
WHOA! SHOW US! SHOW US!

DOESN'T HE SPEAK, LIKE HUMAN LANGUAGES ?!
AMAZING, THESE BROS AND THEIR DEMANDS.
SO PUSHY!

NO WAY...
RIGHT... RIGHT, RIGHT...

YOU LOOK LIKE YOU'RE PULLING THE SAME TRICK AS ONE OF THOSE FAKE TELEPATHS.
ARE YOU REALLY EVEN SAYING ANYTHING RIGHT NOW?

CAN'T HE DO ANYTHING SPECIAL?
ANYWAY, HE'S YOUR SERVANT?
WHA...? NO WAY.
HIS CUTENESS IS NO MATCH FOR A HAMSTER'S.
YEAHHH, I DUNNO... HE'S ABOUT AVERAGE.
OH! HE'S HANGING UPSIDE DOWN!
SURE HE CAN. LIKE THIS...
WHOAAA!
AND HE'S GOOD AT SWOOPING!
WHOOSH
YOU CAN MAKE HIM DO THAT, TOO?!
GLIDE
スィ
HE'S GOOD AT CIRCLING!
スィ GLIDE
WHOAA!
FLAAAP
HE CAN FLY REALLY WELL!
WHOA!
FLAAAP

WHOA... THIS IS THE FIRST TIME I'VE SEEN A BAT UP CLOSE!
THIS IS CRAZY. IT'S SO CALM.
WHAT'S ITS NAME?
THIS IS A JAPANESE SHORT-TAILED BAT. IT USUALLY SITS AROUND THE NECK. USUALLY THEY'RE ABOUT FIVE CENTIMETERS LONG, BUT THIS GUY'S A DOMINANT MALE SO HE'S BIGGER. I MEAN, HE'S DOMINANT, BUT ALSO MY SERVANT.
OH, AND HIS NAME'S URAMI.
CUTE, ISN'T HE?

...LIKE A GIRL WHO SUBTLY CHANGES HER HAIR AND GETS MAD WHEN YOU DON'T NOTICE!
THAT WOULD JUST BE PASSIVE-AGGRESSIVE...
IS WHAT I WANT TO SAY. BUT I CAN'T!
THE VAMPIRE BROUGHT A BAT TO SCHOOL!
BE CARE-FUL!
"WHAT KIND OF CLICHÉ IS THAT?"
FLAP
AH! SOME-THING'S FLYING UP THERE!
IT'S HUGE! IS IT A MOTH?!
FLAP
KA-CLUK
I HAVE TO TAKE DIRECT ACTION!
FLAP
FLAP
KILL IT! KILL IT!
NO! STOP...!

BA-BUM
BA-BUM
THE NEXT AFTER-NOON.
BING
キーン
BONG
コーン
SQUEE!
ワイ
SQUEE!
ワイ
KYA HA HA!
CHITTER
ガヤ
CHATTER
ガヤ
UGH, THESE BROS! IT'S LIKE TIME FLOWS DIFFER-ENTLY FOR THEM.
THEY DO HAVE A LOT GOING ON IN THEIR LIVES.
THEY FORGOT!

AH... THEY SEEM... UNINTER-ESTED
UHHHH... YEAH.
WHOOSH
WHOOSH
THAT'S BECAUSE LIVING THIS LONG IS, IN ITSELF, A SIN.
WITH A LONG LIFE, YOU ACCRUE A LOT OF KARMA, RIGHT?
IT'S LIKE POWER DERIVED FROM YOUR SINS.
BY KARMA, I MEAN THE KIND YOUR SOUL BUILDS UP OVER TIME.
IN SHORT, I'M TOO YOUNG...
...HAVE A BAT AS A SUBORDI-NATE.
ACTUALLY, I DO...
HE'S LYING
I... DON'T SEE WHY NOT?
AW, CRAP.
I WANNA SEE!
BRING IT IN!
YEAH! BRING IT TOMOR-ROW!
KOIDE, YOU'RE AMAZING!
WHOA! REALLY?!

WELL, YOU SEE... I HAVEN'T AMASSED ENOUGH KARMA.
"KARMA"? WHAT'S THAT?
Chapter 4
1st Week of July (134th time)

BUT JUST AS IT LOOKED LIKE I'D BE ALONE FOREVER ...
YO, VAMPIRE! GO BUY US DESSERT...
...FROM THE CONVENIENCE STORE BY THE TRAIN STATION!
HEY! ME TOO!
BUT... THAT'S TOO FAR!
IT'S A QUICK FLIGHT IF YOU JUST CHANGE INTO A BAT, RIGHT?
I CAN'T DO THAT!
...I SOMEHOW GOT CAUGHT UP WITH THESE GUYS.
YOU CAN'T TRANSFORM? BUT YOU'RE A VAMPIRE.
VAMPIRES GENERALLY CAN...
...I JUST CAN'T.
WHY NOT?

HIIIISS!!

WOW... HE'S REALLY MAD!
HUHR!

AND THE GIRLS' HATRED OF ME RE-DOUBLED.
YOU'RE AWFUL!
KODE, YOU'RE THE WORST!
.....
S-SORRY... I JUST... DON'T LIKE DOGS.
I MADE THE GIRL NEXT TO ME FEAR FOR HER LIFE...

I AM A VAMPIRE.
SINCE I'M IMMORTAL, I HAVE HAD TO REPEAT, OVER AND OVER, MY FIRST YEAR OF HIGH SCHOOL. (OR SECONDARY SCHOOL, AS IT WAS KNOWN IN THE OLD SYSTEM.)

HER NAME'S NICHI-NICHI!
SHE'S A POMERA-NIAN!

HEY, KOIDE-KUN!
LOOK, LOOK! THIS IS MY DOGGIE!

ARE YOU REALLY LOOKING? COME ON.
.....

LOOK! LOOK!
SHOVE
SHOVE

ISN'T SHE CUTE?
Y... YEAH...

HOLLY

VAMPIRES ESPECIALLY HATE CERTAIN PLANTS, INCLUDING HOLLY, ASPEN, AND WILD ROSES.

HOLLY'S THORNY LEAVES REPRESENT CHRIST'S SUFFERING, AND ITS BERRIES REPRESENT THE BLOOD OF CHRIST.

BEING HIT WITH A WHIP MADE OF HOLLY IS EXTREMELY PAINFUL FOR VAMPIRES—AND FOR HUMANS.

BUT FOR VAMPIRES, THEIR WOUNDS REMAIN FOR ETERNITY.

AH...! YOUR TRUNKS ARE SLIPPING!!

CHAPTER 3 / END

ITS DELICIOUS FLAVOR IS REVOLUTIONARY.
THIS CHICKEN, FRIED TO PERFECTION IN HIGH-PRESSURE COOKERS AND FLAVORED WITH ELEVEN HERBS AND SPICES...

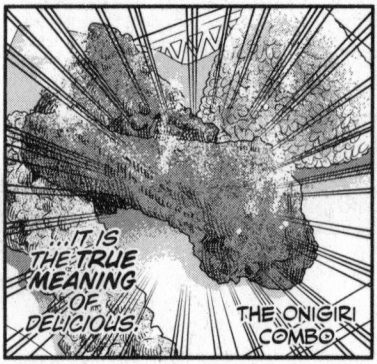
...IT IS THE TRUE MEANING OF DELICIOUS!
THE ONIGIRI COMBO

ほわ～
TENDER AND JUICY...
THE FEELING OF PULLING THAT MEAT APART...
ITS SOFT, AROMATIC COATING...

COMPARISON CHART
OLDEST
MIURA (1572-)
KOIDE (1864-)
THE COLONEL (1890- 1980)
YOUNGEST

1,280 YEN ($12.80 USD) FOR 45 MINUTES IN HEAVEN.
ALL YOU CAN EAT!
WE MAKE RESERVATIONS FOR THE ONCE-A-YEAR, ALL-YOU-CAN-EAT SPECIAL AND GET IN LINE...

※ SELF-CENSORSHIP.

WHAT HAPPENED TO YOUR BACK?

OH, THAT'S FROM WHEN THE FARMERS USED TO BEAT ME DURING THE MIDDLE AGES.
R-REALLY...?

WHAT WERE YOU TWO DOING?
FOR MASS-AGING OUR LEGS.
THANKS, SIR.

NOT TO THE POINT OF CRAMP-ING YOUR LEGS!
SO WE WERE WORKING OFF SOME STRESS.

WE WANTED TO GET IN THE POOL, BUT COULDN'T.
I GUESS IT CAN'T BE HELPED.

IT'S ALL WE'VE EATEN FOR THE LAST THIRTY YEARS.
WE LOVE KEN-CLUCKY FRIED CHICKEN MORE THAN WE CAN SAY.

BY THE WAY, MIURA...
REALLY...? IN THAT CASE, AT LEAST EAT THE COLESLAW.

OUR DIET'S NOT VERY BALANCED. SINCE OUR NUTRIENTS ARE SO RESTRICTED, WE CRAMP EASILY.
WE WEREN'T OVER-WORKING--WE'RE VAMPIRES.

SINCE WE'RE SO WEAK IN THE DAYTIME...

...ONLY AFTER SCHOOL CAN WE BE LIKE THE COUNT.
DRACULA, THAT IS.

WE WERE A BIT BOASTFUL, AND PROBABLY LOOKED DUMB...
...BUT WE ENJOYED OUR-SELVES THERE FOR SOME TIME.

HEY! WE'RE CLOSING UP--
OUR LEGS ARE CRAMP-ED!

MY LEGS ARE CRAMPING!
MY...
I KNEW IT!
AND YOU'RE SO WHITE!
MIURA
THE SUN'S RAYS...!
AND I'M CAUGHT IN...
I'D BETTER ...
SAVE HIM.
FWUP

CLING
CLING
CLING
CLING
CLING
CLING
SLIDE
スイ
SLIIIDE
スイー
IT DOES LOOK LIKE HE'S HAVING FUN...
!
.....
...BUT I'M THE ADULT HERE.

FWU
MP
YOU WANT TO GET IN THE POOL THAT BAD?!
I WORE MY BATHING SUIT UNDER MY SCHOOL UNIFORM.
AND YOU'RE REALLY WHITE!
KOIDE
I FEEL LIKE SWIMMING.
I...KIND OF FEEL SORRY FOR YOU...
HUH?

I WANNA DO THE SWIRLING-AROUND THING, TOO!
BAAAM
.....
AND I WANNA BE THE ONE WHO GOES AGAINST THE CURRENT!!
RUMBLE
RUMBLE
RUMBLE
IT MIGHT LOOK FUN TO YOU... BUT FOR MOST PEOPLE IN CLASS, THAT'S THE MOST BORING THING.
YOU KNOW, ACTU-ALLY...
I...
H-HEY!
SNAP
ZIP
WHAT ARE YOU DOING?!

SO... HOW WAS THE POOL?
I WATCHED FROM THE SHADE, OF COURSE.

ACTUALLY, SOME PRIEST-LIKE GUY WAS CLEANING THE WATER... OR MAYBE HE WAS BLESSING IT.
SO DON'T TOUCH THE POOL WATER, NO MATTER WHAT, OKAY? YOU'LL GET KELOIDS.
WAS TODAY THE POOL'S OPENING DAY?
RICHARD

THOSE GUYS REALLY LOVE GOING IN CIRCLES IN THE POOL.
THEY'RE OBSESSED WITH THE WHIRPOOL, OR WHATEVER IT'S CALLED.

SO AFTER THAT, YOU JUST RAN AROUND?
YEAH. I FELT LIKE AN IDIOT, HAVING A BLAST...
AS USUAL?

WHOSE SIDE ARE YOU ON, MIURA?
THEIR MISCHIEF RAINS DOWN LIKE THE BLOWS OF A BLACK BELT: ONE PRANK AFTER ANOTHER...
LEAVE IT TO THE BROS, THEIR LITTLE HEARTS OVERFLOWING WITH MESSED UP JOKES.
THOSE FARMERS IN THE MIDDLE AGES WERE TERRIBLE.
WELL, THERE'S NO LIMIT TO THE BULLYING OF THE LOWEST CASTE, IS THERE?
OKAY, SORRY, THAT'S ENOUGH.
GROUPTHINK CAN BE POWERFUL...AND DEADLY.
JEEZ... GARBAGE IN, GARBAGE OUT.
150 YEARS OLD.
442 YEARS OLD.
I DON'T WANNA HEAR THIS!!
I WAS BEATEN OVER AND OVER AGAIN...
TRUST ME. HOLLY AND ASPEN SWITCHES LEAVE SERIOUS SCARS.
WHUMP

...AND THAT'S HOW I PULLED OFF A FULL DAY OF ***STEALTH.***

YOUR CLASS-MATES HAVE A **TWISTED** SENSE OF HUMOR.

AMAZING.

HEY, KOIDE, CAN YOU TRY STANDING IN FRONT OF THE WHITE SPACE ON THAT WALL?
HUH? WHY?
WHOA! DID HE DISAPPEAR?
IS HE SO WHITE WE CAN'T SEE HIM?
MAYBE HE ALREADY WENT TO THE POOL?
MAYBE HE DID!
WHERE'D HE GO?
WHERE ARE YOU?

I DON'T HAVE WINGS!
SPEAKING OF WHICH, I'VE BEEN WONDERING... DO YOU EVER WORRY THAT IF YOU TAKE OFF YOUR UNIFORM, PEOPLE WILL SEE THE WINGS ON YOUR BACK?
THESE GUYS SUCK AT STAYING ON THE SUBJECT.

I'M NOT GETTING IN THE POOL...
...SO I'M NOT CHANG-ING.

IF NOT COM-PLETELY WHOLE-SOME!
SHUT UP!

YOU WANNA HAVE A LOOK?
MY SHOULDERS ARE GORGEOUS, YA KNOW?

SO PALE YOU LOOK ALMOST DEAD.
I AM ALMOST DEAD.
YOUR SKIN'S SO NICE, IT'S KINDA EERIE... CAN I TOUCH IT?

DUDE... YOU'RE SO PALE!
YOUR SKIN IS REALLY PALE!

HOW...?
EVEN THOUGH IT'S WATER
HUH...? BURNED...?

SO WATER'S BAD ENOUGH IN ITSELF. BUT WATER CLEANSED WITH *SALT* IS WORSE, SINCE THAT ESSENTIALLY MAKES IT HOLY WATER... SEE, THE POOL HAS CHLORINE, RIGHT? SO, IF A VAMPIRE TOUCHES THAT, THEIR BODY WILL GO "*HSSSS*," AND THEN IT'S "*OWW!*"
LET ME EXPLAIN. WATER IS TRADITIONALLY USED TO WASH AWAY SINFUL THINGS, RIGHT? PEOPLE USE WATER IN BAPTISMS, AND THE BIBLE SAYS A FLOOD SWEPT AWAY ALL THE SINNERS...IN SHORT, WATER IS *SCARY*.

YOU GUYS ARE IN *HIGH SCHOOL!* GET USED TO LONG-FORM CONTENT OR YOU'LL REGRET IT! ALL YOU READ NOW IS *LIGHT NOVELS!!*
C'MON!
YEEAH!
HA HA HA HA!

WHAT? WEREN'T YOU LISTENING?
HUH? KOIDE, YOU'RE NOT TAKING YOUR UNIFORM OFF?

NO... I'LL GET BURNED... IF I TOUCH THE WATER.
THOUGH, IT'S SO HOT OUT, I MIGHT GET BURNED ANYWAY.
Chapter 3
Last Week of June (134th time)

...I'M KEEPING MY DISTANCE. WHO KNOWS WHY.
SELF-LOATHING, MAYBE?

THERE ARE GUYS IN MY CLASS I COULD FIT IN WITH.
AH... I JUST WANNA DIE
ME TOO...
BUT WHILE THEY SEEM GLOOMY ENOUGH ...

ON THE OTHER HAND, THESE GUYS SEEM INTERESTED IN ME.
YO, YO, YO! IT'S SWIM-DAY GYM-DAY!
YO, VAMPIRE! LET'S GO TO THE POOOL!

IT'S NOT A QUESTION OF WHETHER I CAN SWIM.
THEN YOU'LL BE FINE!
RIGHT?
CLATTER

I CAN'T... GO... TO THE POOL.
WHY NOT? SUN'S NOT THAT BRIGHT TODAY.
OH, KOIDE! YOU CAN'T SWIM?!

AHHH... I JUST WANT TO DIE. I REALLY DO.

WHAT'S UP WITH HIM?
WHA...?

...WE JUST GET EVEN MORE DEPRESSED.
BUT INSTEAD, SINCE WE'RE IMMORTAL...

WE GET SO DEPRESSED THAT WE LITERALLY WANT TO DIE.
WE VAMPIRES FIND BRIGHT, SUNNY DAYS EXTREMELY DEPRESSING.

CHAPTER 3 / THE LAST WEEK OF JUNE (134TH TIME)

My Pathetic Vampire Life

MIURA
KOIDE

CHAPTER 2 / END

THAT WAS A SUDDEN SHIFT. AS SOMEONE IN A SIMILAR BOAT, I'M A BIT EMBARRASSED.
JUST... COME WITH ME.
EH HEH...
WHERE ARE WE GOING?
OH? YOU'RE STILL HERE?
DID HE HEAR ANYTHING?
カタッ!
CLATTER
OH, HEY! YOU'RE STILL HERE, KOIDE! COME WITH ME FOR A SEC!
HAVE A SEAT.
H-HUH? WHAT'S UP? YOU'RE ALL HERE?
STILL HAVEN'T GONE HOME, EH?
OHHH, KOIDE!
WHAT IF THEY DID? ARE THEY VENGEFUL? AM I GONNA DIE HERE?!
D-DID THEY HEAR ME TALKING BAD ABOUT THEM?
EVEN THOUGH I CAN'T?!
WH... WHAT?

NOT ME. I'M NOT LIKE THAT.
OF COURSE WE'D TALK BAD ABOUT THEM.
BUT THAT'S OUR *NATURE*, RIGHT? VAMPIRES PREY ON HUMANS.
ALL RIGHT. I UNDER-STAND.
IT'S BECAUSE YOU'RE SO MUCH OLDER THAT I NEED YOU TO HEAR ME OUT.
COME *ONNNN*. WE'RE IN THE SAME BOAT!
ACTUAL AGE: 442
ACTUAL AGE: 150
AND THEIR PERSONALITIES ARE SO... *BRIGHT*. THEY'RE LIKE THE SUN.
AND THAT'S NOT A COMPLIMENT, COMING FROM A VAMPIRE.
EVEN IF YOU *ARE* GOING TO **DIE**, YOU'D WANT PICTURES OF WHEN YOU LIVED.
I GET THAT IF YOU'RE ENJOYING LIFE THAT MUCH, YOU'D WANT PICTURES FOR LATER...
SO THESE BROS *REALLY* LOVE TAKING PICTURES.
AH... LIKE THE OCEAN'S ROARING WAVES. THEY SOUND PROFOUNDLY ANNOYING.

THESE GUYS ARE MORONS.
SOLID! HOW LUCKY ARE WE?!
YE-AH! WE GOT TO SKIP AFTERNOON CLASSES!
BA HA HA HA!
HEY OOO!

1 – 2
THE GUYS IN MY CLASS ARE A BUNCH OF IDIOTS.
AND THERE YOU HAVE IT...

I DON'T SAY BAD THINGS ABOUT THEM TO THEIR FACES.
I CAN'T HELP IT. THE DAYTIME MAKES ME WEAK.
BUT THAT'S HOW IT IS EVERY DAY, RIGHT?

NOW, NOW... TALKING BEHIND THEIR BACKS ISN'T NICE.
MIURA KURARA
16 years old
(426th time)

I NEED TO TAKE ONE MORE!
SORRY, EVERY-ONE.

KA-SNAP
WHAT THE--?
KA-SNAP
LET'S JUST GET ONE MORE ...!

THIS IS STRANGE... CREEPY, EVEN...
WH-WHAT?
IT'S LIKE.. A SPIRIT PHOTO OR SOMETHING.

AAAGH! THIS IS DEFINITELY BECAUSE I'M NOT SHOWING UP!
IS THE CAMERA BROKEN?
CHATTER
CHATTER
CHATTER
WHAAAT?! THIS IS STRANGE, ISN'T IT ...?
HE'S TAKING ANOTHER?
CHATTER

HMMM... TER-RIBLY SORRY...
HOW MANY DID THAT PHOTO-GRAPHER TAKE?
UGH, I'M EX-HAUST-ED.
AW, MAN! IT'S AFTER SCHOOL ALREADY!

S-SERIOUSLY?
WHAT IF THEY'RE RIGHT? THAT'D BE GREAT!
OH, YEAH! IT'LL WORK WITH DIGITAL!
MODERN TECHNOLOGY IS AMAZING!
REALLY? SO THAT'S THE ISSUE?
SURE! AS LONG AS WE GET YOU IN FOCUS!
ALL RIGHT... HERE WE GO!
SMIIILE!
KA-SNAP

THEY THOUGHT I WAS JUST ABSENT, SO THEY TOOK IT AGAIN. BUT I STILL DIDN'T SHOW UP... WHICH MADE IT A PRETTY TERRIBLE PICTURE.
I THINK I SAW SOMETHING LIKE THAT ON A TV SHOW ABOUT GHOSTS!
BUT... MODERN CAMERAS SHOULD BE ABLE TO PICK YOU UP, RIGHT?
WHAT?
LIKE, DIGITAL ONES?
Y-YOU THINK ...?
I WAS BORN IN THE MEIJI ERA, SO I'M NOT REALLY UP TO SPEED WITH ALL THIS TECH STUFF.

HEY, DON'T PHOTOGRAPH ME WITHOUT PERMISSION! I HAVE LEGAL RIGHTS TO MY LIKENESS! LEGAL RIGHTS!
YOU DON'T NEED RIGHTS. YOU'RE NOT SHOWING UP ANYWAY.
KA-CLIK
IT'S THE BEGINNING OF APRIL AND THIS IS ALREADY HOW EVERYONE MESSES WITH ME, EVERY DAY.
DO ONE WITH ME, TOO!
ME TOO, ME TOO!
OKAY! NOW TAKE A PIC WITH ME...
I JUST STAY OUT OF THE PICTURE EVERY YEAR.
WHAT ARE YOU GONNA DO?
ISN'T IT CLASS PICTURE DAY?!
WAIT!
...BUT OF COURSE, I DIDN'T SHOW UP.
I TRIED GETTING IN ONCE, ABOUT TWENTY YEARS AGO...

KA-CLIK
カシャッ

SO PEOPLE LIKE YOU ACTUALLY EX!ST?!
WELL... YOU LENT ME YOUR MIRROR AND ALL...
THEN WHY DID YOU PRETEND YOU DID?!
IT WAS ALL AN ACT!
YOU'RE LIVIN' THE BAT-LIFE INSTEAD OF THE BRO-LIFE!

THE CAMERA'S NOT PICKING YOU UP EITHER!
WHOOOA, KOIDE!

IT'S BEEN FOREVER SINCE I'VE SEEN MY OWN FACE.

YES, IT'S TRUE...
THAT'S CRAAAA-ZY!
OH, MAN! IT'S NOT!

HUH?
...BUT DID YOU KNOW YOU HAVE TOOTH-PASTE ON YOUR FACE?

OTHER SIDE! OTHER SIDE! USE THE MIRROR!

HERE'S A MIRROR.
CHECK IT OUT.
OH... THANKS...
SHF

SO VAMPIRES BRUSH THEIR TEETH TOO, HUH?
SOME OF MY TEETH ARE A BIT WEIRD.

IT'S TRUE.
I DON'T SHOW UP IN MIRRORS.

OH, MAN! KOIDE'S NOT BEING REFLECTED IN THE MIRROR!
WHAT?! THAT'S FREAKY!

RIGHT ABOUT HERE.
1ST TIER
2ND TIER
3RD TIER
SWOOP
SWOOP
WHAT'S HIS PROBLEM?
OH, HIM? HE'S A VAMPIRE.
...IN HIGH SCHOOL, OUR POSITION IS MORE PRECARIOUS.
KOIDE MANSAKU
16 years old
(134th time)
Chapter 2
2nd Week of April
(134th time)
THE BRO CROWD IS ALL OVER ME THIS YEAR.
I'LL PASS...THE SUN'S TOO BRIGHT TODAY.
DUDES! LET'S ROLL!
LET'S EAT LUNCH OUTSIDE, YE-EAH!
HE-Y, KOID-E!
WOOOOO
OOKAAAY, BUT...
I'M SORRY TO SAY THIS WHEN YOU'RE IN A BAD MOOD, BUT...

CHAPTER 2 / 2ND WEEK OF APRIL (134TH TIME)

MY PATHETIC VAMPIRE LIFE
THE GOVERNMENT'S POSITION ON VAMPIRES
TEENAGE VAMPIRES ARE SENT TO SCHOOL TO KEEP THEM FOCUSED ON STUDIES AND OFF THE STREETS. IN OTHER WORDS, TO KEEP THEM FROM TERRORIZING THE PUBLIC AT LARGE.
ER
IF VAMPIRES DON'T ATTEND SCHOOL, THE GOVERNMENT—WORKING CLOSELY WITH ITS CONTRACTOR, HELSING CORP.—HUNTS THEM DOWN.

THE TRANSFER OF ENERGY

BUT NO ONE'S AROUND TO SEE, BECAUSE IT'S NIGHT.

CHAPTER 1 / END

YO! KOIDE!
CHATTER
CHATTER
1-1

UH...
YEEEEAH!
WEATHER'S GREAT! LET'S GO PLAY SOCCER!

MAYBE THESE GUYS ARE IDIOTS?
YOU MEAN YOU FORGOT I ALMOST DIED?
AND "WEATHER'S GREAT" IS HIGHLY SUBJECTIVE.

LOOK, I HAD THIS LYING AROUND. TAKE IT, IT'S YOURS.
YEAHHH, I THOUGHT YOU MIGHT SAY THAT!
UM, HEY... MAYBE YOU FORGOT, BUT... VAMPIRES CAN'T BE IN SUNLIGHT.

I DON'T WANNA GO TO SCHOOL ANYMORE.
WHY? IS YOUR HEART BROKEN BECAUSE IBUKI-SAN GAVE YOU A HARD TIME FOR BEING SCARED?
NO. WELL, THAT'S PART OF IT.
I JUST WONDER, WHY DO WE EVEN GO TO SCHOOL...
...IF IT JUST MEANS MISERABLE EXPERI-ENCES LIKE THESE?
.....
IT CAN'T BE HELPED. WE HAVE TO GO.
IF WE DON'T, THE GOVERN-MENT WILL HUNT US DOWN.
YEAHHH... THAT'S TRUE.
IT'S NOT EASY BEING US.

SENSEI! GET IT!
GET THE DOG!
A-ALL RIGHT...
H-HEY! COME BACK HERE!

I TRIED TO GRAB IT, BUT IT GOT AWAY.
OH, UH, YEAH...
DO YOU KNOW WHERE IT WENT?
OH, BY THE WAY... I HEARD THERE WAS A DOG AROUND HERE EARLIER.
BAP
BAP
BAP
BAP
BAP
OHHHH ...

YOU KNOW I'M OLDER THAN YOU... RIGHT, TEACH?
UHH...
WHAT A WEAK GYM TEACHER, BUCKLING AS SOON AS HIS SUPERIORITY IS QUESTIONED.

WELL, WHY DO YOU NEED TO BUY BAKED GOODS?
SO THERE'S NO NEED FOR YOU TO GO, RIGHT?
VAMPIRES DON'T EAT THOSE.

THE GUYS FROM CLASS ASKED ME TO.
SO TURN THEM DOWN.
KOIDE

NO WAY COULD I DO THAT!
YOU HAVE SENIORITY, DON'T YOU?!

SHEESH... JUST BE CAREFUL GOING HOME, OKAY?
OKAY...

WHY WEREN'T YOU IN CLASS TODAY?!
AND, KOIDE!
HEY, WE'RE CLOSING UP THE BUILDING!
OKAAY!
WELL, BE MORE CAREFUL, WOULD YA?
YOU SEE, I WAS CAUGHT IN THE SUN AND COLLAPSED.
YOU'VE GOT THE WRONG IDEA, SIR.
CLATTER ガラ
CLATTER ガラ
THAT'S A HEAVY LOAD, CONSIDERING THE REST OF YOUR DAYS GO ON FOR ETERNITY.
PLEASE. I'LL OWE YOU FOR THE REST OF MY DAYS.
I DON'T HAVE THAT KIND OF PULL.
SAY, TEACH? COULD YOU PLEASE ASK THEM TO PUT A ROOF OVER THE WALKWAY, SO I CAN GO BUY PASTRIES?

SIGH... I JUST DON'T GET WHY WE... WHO ARE SUPPOSEDLY AT THE TOP OF THE FOOD CHAIN...
...JUST DRIFT BETWEEN THE SECOND AND THIRD TIERS OF OUR SCHOOL, LIKE MERE BIT PLAYERS?
VAMPIRES
1ST TIER
2ND TIER
3RD TIER
この辺
HERE-ISH
SWOOP キョロ
SWOOP キョロ

I SAW A MOVIE RECENTLY ...
...IN WHICH THE VAMPIRE, THREATENED BY HIS ENEMY, CLING TO THE CEILING.

WE VAMPIRES HAVE BEEN MOCKED FROM THE START.
AND MAYBE WE SHOULD BE. WE MAY NOT BE THAT INTERESTING.
SIGH...

THEY DO MOCK US, DON'T THEY...?
I'VE NEVER CLUNG TO THE CEILING. NOT ONCE.

MY CLASS-MATES SEEM TO THINK I'M THEIR SUBORDI-NATE THIS YEAR.
OH? THAT'S NO GOOD.

OH! AND SPEAKING OF DOGS ...

I MEAN, THEY CARE FOR ME...JUST IN THE WAY THEY WOULD FOR A DOG...
KOIDE. YOU'RE FINE.

IF THAT'S YOUR ONLY PROB-LEM, YOU'RE FINE.
YOU WEREN'T AROUND IN THE MIDDLE AGES. BACK THEN, WE WERE PERSECUTED EVEN ON SUSPICION OF BEING VAMPIRES.
I'M JUST GRATEFUL THAT THESE GUYS ACCEPT US.

GRRRR!
IF ONLY SCHOOL WERE HELD AT NIGHT, I'D MAKE THOSE BASIC BROS MY SUBORDI-NATES!
BUT OF COURSE, SCHOOL'S DURING THE DAY...

...SO EVERY DAY THERE I AM, WAGGING MY TAIL.
WAGGING YOUR TAIL?! DON'T TELL ME YOU WANT THEM TO LIKE YOU!

I HATE DOGS AS WELL.
I AM A VAMPIRE, AFTER ALL.
I AM A VAMPIRE, AFTER ALL.
BESIDES! I HATE DOGS.

OUR BORN ENEMIES.
THE WOLF-TYPE DOGS?
SHUDDER
SHUDDER

THAT BREED ...
ESPE-CIALLY HUSKIES?
SHUDDER
SHUDDER

AGREED. SHIBAS ARE MUCH TOO CLOSE TO WOLVES.
BUT I CAN'T STAND SHIBA-INU!
ARRRRRRRRRRR

YES. THEY'RE CUTE, CLEVER, AND DON'T SHED SO BAD.
TOY POODLE
I DO LIKE TOY POODLES A LITTLE.

YOU'RE HARD TO PLEASE, AREN'T YOU?
EVEN THOUGH THE WHOLE THING'S *REALLY* LAME.

YOU'RE SO NICE, MIURA.
WELL, WHAT CAN YOU DO? FOR THEM IT PROBABLY IS THE FIRST TIME.
ACTUAL AGE: 150 YEARS OLD
ACTUAL AGE: 442 YEARS OLD

THEY GO ON ABOUT IT LIKE IDIOTS. THIS *BIG THING* THAT HAPPENED AT THE BEGINNING OF THEIR HIGH SCHOOL YEARS.
BUT FOR ME, THIS HAS ALREADY HAPPENED... *SO MANY TIMES.*

NO. I JUST WANT SOME PEACE AND QUIET THIS TIME AROUND.

WE'VE BEEN FRIENDS FOR AROUND 130 YEARS.
COINCI-DENTALLY, THERE'S ANOTHER VAMPIRE IN THE NEXT CLASS OVER.

DID YOU GET ALONG WITH YOUR CLASSMATES TODAY?
HOW WAS IT?
MIURA KURARA
16 years old
(426th time)

IT CAUSED QUITE A STIR.
THEY SAID A DOG GOT INTO THE CLASS-ROOM TODAY.

I TALKED WITH MINE A LOT.
MEH. SO-SO.
ガリ
SCRAPE

あはは
AHHAHHA!
YOU GOT BARKED AT!
YEAH WELL, Y'KNOW...
YET, FOR SOME REASON, I FEEL LIKE THIS TIME AROUND... THINGS ARE GOING TO BE OKAY.

あはは
AH HA HA HA HA!
WHAT WERE YOU DOING ?!
WE TOLD YOU TO BE CARE-FUL, DIDN'T WE?!
YOU GOT CAUGHT IN THE SUN!

...A DOG GOT INTO THE CLASS-ROOM!
OH, YEAH! AND WHILE YOU WERE GONE...

KOIDE, YOU MISSED ALL YOUR AFTERNOON CLASSES. THE TEACH-ERS WERE LOOKING FOR YOU.

I'M ALWAYS FAINT AROUND MIDDAY. WEAK. DELICATE.
THIS GUY HERE TRIED TO PET IT!
NO, THAT WAS YOU!
HIGH SCHOOL LIFE CARRIES WITH IT SO MANY HARDSHIPS.
AHA HA HA HA!

AFTER SCHOOL.
キンコーン
BING BOOONG
キンコーン
BEENG BOONG
HE'S LAAATE... HOME-ROOM'S ALREADY OVER.
HOW LONG DOES IT TAKE TO GO BUY LUNCH?
WHICH REMINDS ME: I'M HUNGRY!
ガラッ
H-HEY! THIS IS BAD!
KOIDE PASSED OUT ON HIS WAY HERE!
DASH
ダッ
WHAT ?!
AHH! HE DID!

THIS IS THE STORY OF MY 134TH TIME...
I DON'T LIKE BEING ALONE, SO I HANG OUT WITH THEM ANYWAY.
Chapter 1
3rd Week of June
134th time
KOIDE MANSAKU
16 years old
(134th time)

BECAUSE I'VE WOUND UP IN THAT CASTE MANY TIMES BEFORE.
...BUT I KEEP MY DISTANCE.
IS A WAR VETERAN, SO KNOWS A LOT ABOUT BATTLESHIPS AND AIRCRAFT CARRIERS.

I HAVE SOME TYPICALLY GLOOMY CLASSMATES, WITH WHOM I'M SURE I COULD FIT IN...
THE KAGA WITHDRAWS DUE TO SERIOUS DAMAGE...
MORE THAN THAT...
THERE'S SOMETHING DAUNTING ABOUT SINKING SUCH A RARE CHARACTER.
BAM
BAM

AND THEN THERE'S THE REST OF THEM... THE ONES WHO ARE SATISFIED IN THE REAL WORLD.
HE-Y, VAMPIIIRE! GO GET US SOME JUUUICE!
PASTRIES FOR ME!
I'M NOT SO GOOD WITH THEM.

BUT...

YEAH, BUT, SEE... IF I GO OUTSIDE, I'LL BE EXPOSED TO THE SUN...
GET ME SOME TOO, KOIDE!
ウェーイ!
EY!
.....

YOU DO KNOW HIGH SCHOOL'S NOT THAT INTERESTING, RIGHT?

CHAPTER 1 / 3RD WEEK OF JUNE (134TH TIME)

I'M A VAMPIRE.

I STOPPED AGING AT **SIXTEEN** AND HAVE HAD TO **REPEAT** MY FIRST YEAR OF HIGH SCHOOL IN A VICIOUS CYCLE EVER SINCE.

YEP, I'M THE REAL DEAL...

WHOA! I GET TO SIT NEXT TO THE VAMPIRE!

...WHICH MADE THE GIRL WHO SAT NEXT TO ME ON THE FIRST DAY **VERY** HAPPY.

SITTING NEXT TO A VAMPIRE ON MY FIRST DAY! I'M *SOOO* LUCKY!

LOOKS LIKE IT'LL BE AN INTERESTING THREE YEARS! NICE TO MEET YOU, **KOIDE-KUN**.

AHEM. SO...

I'VE BEEN THROUGH THIS A FEW TIMES, AND... WELL...

ENOUGH! NO MATTER HOW MANY YEARS PASS, ONE TRUTH REMAINS: MY HIGH SCHOOL LIFE ALWAYS SUCKS!
THAT'S BEFORE MY TIME!
I WASN'T EVEN BORN YET!
AT LEAST IT WAS NICE IN 19TH CENTURY LONDON. THE AIR POLLUTION WAS SO THICK FROM THE SECOND INDUSTRIAL REVOLUTION, WE COULDN'T EVEN SEE THE SUN.
150 YEARS OLD.
442 YEARS OLD.
...MIGHT SOMEHOW END UP... NOT SUCKING.
BUT... FOR SOME REASON...I FEEL LIKE THIS TIME...
AHHH! I CAN'T TAKE IT!
NOW I DON'T WANNA TALK TO ANYONE TODAY!
VRRRRRM
AH, HERE COMES THE BUS.
ピカー
CLINT